1. Coronets & Bonnets

Love flies on wordy wings, blessed with God's speed.
Air-borne, ethereal, yet earthy sonnets,
Speak oral, free from a corral, glib steed
Rushing to their destiny. Coronets
And bonnets upon ladies heads give birth
To phrases, lines – romantic dialect
For their fancies, philosophy and mirth.
How to embellish their keen intellect?
How to stir their hearts, minds, souls for applause?
Fertilize their pretty heads with fecund
Matters, plant seeds not weeds of thought, for pause.
Eternity is a timeless beyond,
Captured well by literary content,
Approved by writers, muses, fans consent.

2. Bastard Bowdlerism

Curse on any who dare to bowdler*ize*,
These works in memory of the great *Bard*,
Who raised the English from a bastard*ized*
Pleasantry to the Queen's fine language. *Guard*
Well these words without any censorsh*ip*;
They will stand true, correct, without a *gyp*.
Those good few who dare, may give voice or *lip*
To these, timeless as pyramids of *Egypt*.
This magnum opus worthy of *genius*,
Shall be studied by each English sch*olar*.
Classified in its own sonnet *genus*,
It is worth each pound, peso, or *dollar*.
These sundry sonnets deserve praise and *laud*;
Thus, generous, kind readers please app*laud*!

3. Willing Wittols

Quadrangle character play to beh<u>old</u>,
Written in these sonnets. Playful four<u>some</u>
Romp, literally to make a cuck<u>old</u>
Or two... A sense of humour for whole<u>some</u>
Adult interaction: pretty actr<u>ess</u>,
With two awards, beautiful, stalwart Qu<u>een</u>
Witty, versatile, pleasing poet<u>ess</u>
And handsome, religious artist from sc<u>ene</u>
One. All four play-acting the com<u>edy</u>
Drama of adultery. Tear-jerk<u>er</u>
It is not: no depressing trag<u>edy</u>
To weep by, nor romantic disast<u>er</u>
To remember. It's a weird play of sp<u>oil</u>
Indulge love, become a willing witt<u>ol</u>...

4. Visiting The Queen

How quick my fawning heart capitul<u>ates</u>
To her high-born ways! Gone my poor <u>sadness</u>,
As to her charms I fall. She capti<u>vates</u>
Women, men, children with loyal gl<u>adness</u>.
Angels soar on Her Holy Be<u>atitudes</u>!
Wisdom and grace attire this royal s<u>aint</u>.
Some attain honourable <u>attitudes</u>,
Though I confess at sight of her, I'd f<u>aint</u>!
Romantic admiration hibern<u>ate</u>
As I dream in Canada's Winter <u>Sun</u>
Shall my will and body recupe<u>rate</u>
When She blesses this vast, promised Can<u>aan</u>?
Of if Heaven would crown the King as <u>keen</u>,
'To London, to London, visit the <u>Queen</u>!

5. American Lioness

If with my faded youth I would pre<u>sume</u>,
To dream about such magnetic form, gr<u>ace</u>,
Would not my simple soul and mind a<u>ssume</u>
Beauty, love, intelligence has a f<u>ace</u>?
An American lioness on-scr<u>een</u>,
Caged tense on high, she surpasses her cl<u>ass</u>!
Leaving all to ponder what she might m<u>ean</u> --
The eager, curious cinematic m<u>ass</u>.
How ever does she do it one may <u>ask</u>?
Shedding each character, role, mood on st<u>age</u>
As in a costumer ball one dons a m<u>ask</u>
Parading like a princess, all the r<u>age</u>.
Down below we wait watching but con<u>fused</u>
By this entrancing, mesmerizing M<u>use</u>.

6. Honey Bear

Hairy bears are fond of sweet, rich h<u>oney</u>.
They amble around forests full of f<u>ur</u>.
Though neither of us have lots of m<u>oney</u>,
We laugh, love, live! Does it ever occ<u>ur</u>
To you to improve our peaceful home l<u>ife</u>?
Often contentment fills us, my best fr<u>iend</u>.
Yes, I would agree to be your housew<u>ife</u>,
If you will be my husband. Till the <u>end</u>,
We will be together, my mag<u>ician</u>
As partners, a laddie to his b<u>onnie</u>.
Two water signs, we'll swim in the <u>ocean</u>
Of life, discovering truths, not ph<u>oney</u>
Lies that split us apart. With a tear<u>ful</u>
Embrace, we will share all that is joy<u>ful</u>!

7. Maestro's Muses

Inspired by Muses, conducts the Maestro
Magnificent poetry from mael<u>stroms</u>
Of words and emotions. No fias<u>co</u>
Performances, destructive as bad <u>storms</u>,
Shall wreck her orchestration. Each m<u>oody</u>
Whim written in wonder of her heart-thr<u>obs</u>,
Steers her pen. No drab metaphor, <u>dowdy</u>
Or dull shall incite loud rallies from m<u>obs</u>,
Thronging with longing for mental i<u>dols</u>;
Thrilling crowds in fervent exalt<u>ation</u>,
Her pen's mightier than the sword! For <u>dolls</u>,
She writes, straining in exasper<u>ation</u>
For the apt word, wanting to en<u>amor</u>
Her avid fans too with a par<u>amour</u>.

8. Royal Sun

As I behold Her, so does the sun ri<u>se</u>.
With my life's breath, I owe to Her a d<u>ebt</u>.
Night's gloom and doom gladly I ostrac<u>ize</u>,
For Her mind's light banishes the sun<u>set</u>.
Words like wind, powerful poetry del<u>uge</u>
My imagination entrances, all<u>ured</u>;
Of Her sins, not one ignoble ink sm<u>udge</u> --
Snow Queen, thy purity has thou in<u>ured</u>!
Thy bearing and wisdom ineff<u>able</u>
In sundry, erudite subjects stu<u>died</u>;
Witty, humorous, find delect<u>able</u>
As mincemeat, each foolish vainglorious <u>deed</u>.
Thy life's story contains no errat<u>um</u>
As perfect as the dawn's memorand<u>um</u>!

9. Marrying In Faith

That we shall marry I believe with <u>faith</u>;
You have opened this matrimonial <u>road</u>.
A voice foretold twelve years ago this <u>fate</u>,
That you and I shall live in one ab<u>ode</u>.
Two become One in metamorph<u>osis</u>,
Forever leaving single life err<u>ant</u>.
How frightening marital mei<u>osis</u>,
If it were not with you, my bear bouf<u>fant</u>!
Shall we cavort blissfully in Ed<u>en</u> --
Playing in God's artistic Cre<u>ation</u>,
Away from all cruel, violent m<u>en</u>
Who tortured real life, imagin<u>ation</u>?
In Holy Union, our propri<u>ety</u>
Shall lead us to form our own soci<u>ety</u>.

10. Romantic Dilettante

Ask of love, oh romantic dilettante,
As one who can cast one cold, heartless hex;
You devour men, voracious ruminant
Like a cow gone mad; we wonder who's next
For dinner, rabid in your distemper?
Perhaps in love, you are quite merciless;
Lacking pity, you selfishly pamper
Your ego with paramours to excess.
Even in friendship, I find you fickle,
Nimble, quick, volatile, unfaithful nymph!
Tease, you tempt me like light feathers tickle,
Primping like a whore for a prudish pimp.
But if you learned fidelity, my flirt
And sauntered off without me, would I hurt?

11. Flutter-by Valentine

Flowers smile at flutter-by coquetry,
Guilty for fawning on a femme fatale.
Several illustrious lines of poetry
Shall be written online ere withdrawal,
Ode to a memorable Valentine.
Saints in faithful love ecumenical
Bond perpetual, unlike a serpentine
Coil deadly striking economical
To the throbbing veins, the nerves that shudder.
Reptilian skin doubtfully get goose bumps
As do polished politicians stutter.
And yet, I lie to say not, my heart pumps
For a glance, a word of inequity
Full of foolish, romantic impiety!

12. Fine Dahlia

If women would remain as girls, dainty,
Would I not give hours and words to dally,
Devoting worship to be a saintly
Play-acting member of the family?
Oh, that you'd look up at me imperious,
As if mistaking me your slave to pose
Generous, kind... driving me delirious
With fascination for you to impose!
Oh, please dear God, on my knees I do pray
That Eden shall sprout such a find dahlia
Who in lasting youth shall prettily prey
On poets and artists melancholia,
Allowing us this mild melodrama
Straining our medulla oblongata!

13. Eulogy For A Eunuch

God rest my suffering form in eulogy,
"Th'unrequited passion of a eunuch,
Faithful servant to your histology,
Here lies resting, finally out of luck."
This fan obsessed by your histrionics
Looks upon Life with sad fatalism.
Indeed, God's great plan entailed bionics:
Diverse, complex, colourful fauvism
In you, quite apparent; no phrase hackneyed
Describes you even post-lobotomy!
No vanquished vessel you, for a man's seed
Body and soul torn in dichotomy,
Farewell physique, have mercy dear clergy,
Lay my body to rest in liturgy.

14. Sisterhood Brotherhood Collusion

'Tis with delicacy and shy finesse,
We discuss love's fashion elaborate.
Yes, nature can follow and yet digress
From the straight and narrow, and celebrate
Love between two women who but comply
To inner yearnings; no, we cannot blame
A strong bond of sisterhood and deny
Man's brotherhood which is above all shame!
Accomplices, we shall in collusion
Deny all wrongs, all disasters avert
In favour, approve such a solution.
'Tis but a pained memory to pervert
Beautiful women into hideous hags;
If it's so, then all such men are but fags.

15. Queen's Deponent

I testify in truth many troubles,
Experiences of commoners, riff raff,
The middle class, and the wealthy's foibles.
You know much about all, royal giraffe
Seeing from above, the bad Gehenna --
The common ground which I, as deponent,
Accede as multi-coloured verbena.
Beloved by most subjects, no opponent,
Thou bewitches us without aversion.
Glorious honour grace faces dolorous;
Thy faithful flock in mass adoration!
Swarming bees to scents non-malodorous
Gleefully enjoying euthanasia
Of their foolish, wayward ways, Dei Gratia!

16. Domesticated Meek

Like domesticated cows are the meek,
Praying salvation in invocation.
What remedy from their lives could they seek?
Perhaps a sign or illumination
That stops the mortal wound of some dagger,
Ends victimization from felony,
As a futile finale with stagger?
How ironic this dreamland colony:
Rich become poor, good incorrigible...
Madness presents such a strange dilemma.
Th' educated's writing's illegible!
What if such grown children's anathema
Will be avoid the bullish bearded brute
Who chases cows in passionate pursuit?

17. Gangster Moll

Made-up moll of some Hollywood gangster,
Poor rape victim, and cold cannibal's shrink --
Roles that you play with a steely-eyed stare.
"Someone call the cops to save her!" I fink.
"The girl's pretty enough to set a craze."
Perhaps the censor board will contravene?
Can the crowd and mother be so unfazed?
She's under-aged to be so used, demeaned.
Why? She's almost a California dream!
But, victim of cinematography,
Your celluloid life's taken to extreme.
Were I to rewrite your biography,
You could play the camera's dilettante,
And be High Society's best debutante!

18. Victim's Complaint

Though taboo, surprisingly loquacious
Regarding assault, complained the plaintiff.
"Just how violent, crafty and vicious
Was he to accomplish this heinous shift
From employer friend to raving maniac?
Did he corner you in isolation
To succeed in his drunken, shock attack?
Just how evil was his molestation
Of your person? Shall it merit bribery?
First impression Miss, is he's a dimwit
And remember now, it ain't robbery.
After all you have been through. But please sit.
Your fine expressions are too ethereal,
He must be guilty or unethical."

19. Humiliation Humbles

Wanting to impress, she shopped, dressed with flair,
Trying to catch attention. Full of dread,
Aroused with desire, she wanted to dare
Acquaint herself with her 'crush'. Her feet's tread
Stumbled, her confidence slipped, as her speech
Mumbled and jumbled. Women's intuition
Told her she would triumph if she'd beseech
God's help! Fear of rejection, not fruition
Froze her from making a move. The prospect
Of humiliation scared her! "Merciful
God, can I hold my head up with respect
After failure? My mind is fanciful,
My heart burning for love! Should I approach
Or should I wait for my sweet crush's reproach?"

20. Love's Dialectic

This melodramatic dialectic
Of what you ponder on as beautiful...
A woman enflamed by love electric
Wins every pageant, makes a judge, a fool.
Madonna's nemesis, iconoclast
Of each treasured romantic liaison,
You analyze love's true faces at last.
Shall you cure illusion with your poison?
Allow us glimpses of your neurosis,
As if love builds such a weak foundation.
When I speak love, you smell halitosis
And silence me from this ostentation.
How could a woman in love be ugly?
Nay impossible! Foolish calumny!

21. Queen Of The Hoi Polloi

Welcoming Queen of the Commonwealth world!
Greeting all peoples with smiles and laughter!
You who have travelled, socialized and whirled
Round the globe, averting each disaster,
Has allowed us close, a fancy decoy
Who does not entrap, nor mislead, nor jilt
Us, your faithful followers. You employ
With cultured, educated tongue and lilt
All your charm and skills; not at all phoney
Regarding your true subjects lives with care.
In diverse dialects, we speak euphony
Celebrating our mutual good welfare.
Kind Majesty, we hope you will enjoy
Our humble company, your hoi polloi.

22. Holy Yokel

A peasant in the woods, but a yokel
Has neither care, wealth, fame, status nor mood.
She climbs every peak only to yodel
As loud as she can. Her prime trait is good.
Euphoric, saintly, no one but a dolt,
Can strive for simplicity. She's tedious,
Persevering, generous to a fault!
'Cleanliness being next to ___' fastidious,
Every pot scrubbed, plate scraped, her domicile
Requires shoes off for her carpet's respect.
Speak when spoken to as an imbecile.
A lady one tips hats, in retrospect.
Her soul shines! Each sinful scratch and tarnish,
In Church, with prayers, psalms, and alms varnished.

23. Gossiping Women

How to avoid such a tempting evil
Is a goal we accomplish with a frown.
"She's your enemy." whispers the Devil
"She scatters dangerous seeds to be sown."
Don't we all prefer blessed solitude?
In mingling, people, our souls get dirty.
Let's heed this good advice in gratitude;
No one's clean and innocent past thirty.
Redemption and soul rebirth fallacious:
Holy water's tap, that crouton's a fake;
The wine is juice; one can't be loquacious
While dear St. Joan is burning at the stake!
Gossip, women, is but a catalyst
To sin and sorrow, says this fatalist.

24. Friend Enemy

Farewell dearest friend of the fair weather!
Skies, heaven are cloudy with deception
All from a mispronounced, misspelled letter.
Have we wasted all our keen perception
Only to shatter friendship with clatter?
Each smile, now a frown, each truth, now a lie --
Witty conversation is but chatter!
I hesitate to breathe, let alone sigh.
Perhaps this misunderstanding, I hate
To say, seems final enough to end love.
Strangers become friends then enemies; fate
Twisted, decrees to be mean when behooved.
How awful that a once treasured friend's cries
Sound shrill and annoying to be despised!

25. Choices Of Temptations

Life's many roads and highways provide choice
Of experiences and people who lure,
Tempting us with many a vivid voice
And colour; our true love once quite secure,
Now unstable as sand. This cruel game
Of who is 'bent' or 'straight' brings no relief.
We need not hang our confused heads in shame.
Romantic monogamy and belief
Of heterosexuality's heartbreak
At multiple partners – a faithful fool
Neither you nor I. Others we awake,
Over our curious eyes, we pull sheep's wool.
No thoughts nor worries of what ever lasts;
We embrace numerous futures and pasts.

26. Domestics Muse

We honour in rhyme, muse emeritus,
Those worthy to incite our souls in forte.
Poetry sublime, not wordy detritus,
Inspires, delicious as a fancy torte!
Shall we joust in some verbal tournament,
Arousing ourselves from catalepsy
To decorate a brilliant ornament?
Clear bouts of poetic epilepsy
Uplifts us to literacy genteel.
In tense, we in lyrical conference,
Aspire to build poems, bold towers of feel,
Pyramids of romantic reverence.
How fantasies enflame in domestic
People, a grandeur superb, majestic!

27. Family Birthright

Many years, family, upon me dote
Concerned and loving enough to invoke
Fidelity; blood is thicker, please note,
Than water. Battles lost and won provoke
Vendettas. Yet, family in epic
Bonded, sprung from one maternal belly;
The original wound anti-septic
Bred us forth, feeding us royal jelly.
Milking like grateful calves, we edify
Our loves, most primary our dear mother.
Those most like her, we respect, deify,
Honouring high, as with our dear father.
Shall we reveal our faithfulness forthright
Proud and noble as we are in birthright?

28. Written Laundry

Feelings are wrung, as well-written laundry,
Hanging for all eyes to see. This fountain
Pen's eloquent, as a sword in foundry,
Sharp and skilled in word play. Reason maintain
Your logic as we rouse from lethargy.
Duty, keep us homebound; we but market
Publicity as we have energy.
We cook for famished masses a banquet
Of poetry and prose, spreading non-profane
Word-foods, as colourful as tongue-dyed clothes.
Maybe beautiful girls driven insane
Shall listen, cheer, applauding as she scolds
As a loud, shrieking and scornful Scorpio
Does well in her shameless amor propio.

29. Wet Dream

Pondering upon her, we do puzzle
Why she, unknown to us, like memories
Imagined, as a wet dream can tousle
Hair, tortures our souls? Lovers have worries.
Doubts spell doomsday for the forbidden friend.
Fantasies play in restricted movies.
Obsessions, to sanatoriums can send
Many a foolish young gay girl who envies
Her own doll, her own cinematic dream.
If we could realize why we now do sigh,
As wild fanatics can stupidly scream
For their indifferent idol on high,
Would sacrificing real life, dear goddess
Make damn heathens of us all and godless?

30. Island Hospitality*

Born in this tropical monsoon island
Sheltered by banana, coconut trees,
"This Earth's Paradise is mine!" I demand.
"In God's Church, I will pray with rosaries
That each typhoon, quake, eruption and storm
Shall cease immediately. All colored fish,
Natives, foreigners, tourists shall conform
To tribal laws. If offered a home dish --
Roast pig, blood stew -- in camaraderie
Everyone must feast to avoid world wars.
Let this modern jungle be sanctuary;
We'll display hospitality in bars.
Entertain yourselves in our cheap burlesque;
Have fun, relax! It is so picturesque!"

* Editor's Choice Award 2001
International Library Of Poetry

31. Border Crossings

Crossing US-Mex border, eureka!
There's so much land for our own hacienda.
All the red peppers to make paprika
A daily addenda in merienda.
Down south, Mother Mary immaculate
Shall intercede and may forgive our sins,
From fatal diseases, inoculate
And release us to eat dangerous shark fins.
The problem lies in crossing this border;
Many die dreaming of this migration,
Shot to death like deer by an officer.
How can one thin line divide each nation?
All we want is to reach the scorching sun;
All we want is to party and have fun!

32. Shattered North

We build permanent dams like a beaver,
Log trees and educate Mother Nature.
The future is bright, one cannot leave her,
This northern country lacking in stature.
Far away enthroned sits the distant Queen,
Signed independence in constitution;
Monarchists wondered why she was so mean,
Severing ties, destroying institution.
Why no public referendum, pow-wow
To decide our fate like whales in Greenpeace?
Every citizen has a vote, knowhow
To choose our citizenship, if we please.
Yet, life lingers progressively up north,
Though shattered people, we must still go forth!

33. Impatient Waiting

Thoughts tumult at seventy megahertz;
Jumbled feelings assault with explosion!
Powerful, turbulent till breathing hurts,
My soul strangled by distant corrosion,
Separated from love ingenuous.
Longing for her gaze inexplicable,
Her quick intelligence so ingenious,
I find reality despicable,
In conversations with others , mordant,
Impatient. Her speech, a revelation
Will be, as I await her abundant
Knowledge, expert in communication.
Can it really be that sad and bizarre
Awaiting her, withdrawn from life's bazaar?

34. Jealousy's Gargoyle

Courtship may end if lovers castigate
Gestures, words from a loving specialist,
Who fools around beyond their faithful gate.
Oh, before love came, we were realists
Grounded in harmless flirtations, reckless.
Jealousy, face of a growling gargoyle
Shelters and guards such stray lovers, feckless
In heart and soul. Oh, that we would recoil
Conscient, from committing such felony.
Shall we in love-wars be dumped by a bitch?
Rivalry in our love's hegemony
Proves a victor; burning chivalry's witch
Hails archaic. Polite euphemisms
For stray partners, but anachronisms.

35. Loneliness Of Lovelessness

Curiously, poetry breeds analgesia;
Perhaps, blocking pain caused by loneliness.
Yet, some recall, forego this amnesia,
Which heals the worn soul with its loveliness.
Oh, that lone despair were ephemeral
Vanishing quick, not plaguing the timid;
Would we in solitary cerebral
Pursuits advance toward the more vivid
Aspects of life? Vibrant is life's strong voice,
Verdant as a forest green, natural
And vast. Shy cowards and meek hear the noise
Ordering death of life, non-liberal,
Confining, full of shushing balderdash,
Cremating both Youth and Elder to ash!

36. Housekeeping Husband

A perfect spouse one can domesticate
With patience and teaching equality
Of genders. To be a potential mate,
One learns housekeeping is a quality
Needed for a happy home and haven!
Men can learn cooking and cleaning. When trained
Well, they appear handsome and clean shaven.
Women adore a home cooked meal, unstained
Laundered sheets, children loved not as burdens
But as treasures. To keep a good balance
Between home and job, both roosters and hens
Must compromise. Avoid mean arrogance
Above domesticity. Contraband
Cleaning marks the ideal loving husband..

37. Royal Tea

In honour, build a royal monument
Of devotion to a queen, observant,
Erudite with charming temperament.
She impresses me much, this humble servant,
With her noble, powerful dignity.
Her ceremonies, comedy-drama,
Serious and gay in world community:
Hear the historical diorama--
"Invite a male political despot
For a wonderful lunch, perhaps a bite
Of delicious cake; with English tea pot
Brew a peaceful revolution, incite
Constitution over a cup of tea.
To refuse, one commits lese majesty."

38. Modern Aunt

With her care, being so felicitous,
I blossomed strong, smart and wise, cheerfully,
Child to woman, she modern, ambitious,
Wore pants, drove, smoked worked and raised us yearly
As her children. Watering us like plants,
She coaxed our growth, healthy in the garden.
It was sad we parted migrant transplants
To Canada, leaving our blood warden:
No more free rides to school from this chauffeur!
No more cool clothes hand sewn by this seamstress!
Room and board, but no coins for her coffer;
Now how could we ever thank her finesse?
We miss her much, virginal, spinster aunt,
Role model, industrious as an ant!

39. alt.showbiz.gossip

Playing mind games with the heart, truth or dare;
Hey, does anyone care? She bewilders
Us ceaselessly; curious cats do beware
Of actresses, nightmare and dream builders.
Movies, of life, make a hullabaloo
Of feelings, scenes, people who titillate
Us strangers, admirers who watch and woo
Filmed stars, who under stage lights scintillate.
Like boot disks that start computers in DOS,
They get our mind gears whirring; on the Net,
Alt.showbiz.gossip opens wide windows
To lies and lives, caught starfish in fishnet.
Today, I shall e-mail her a letter
Applauding her, keeping me in fetter.

40. Eczema Of Love

Warty as a frog prince's skin eczema
Longing for that kiss cure to disinfect
An outcast – romantic anathema
Has banished suitors. Please clearly inspect
Why all beauty and derma went kaput.
Unrequited love makes one eccentric!
Emotions rejected run the gamut,
Despair to elation, an eclectic
Blend causing dermatitis, as of brutes
No one touches. Skin care mumbo jumbo
Masks open wounds, the red pimples of mutes
Who empathize with elephant 'Dumbo'.
Can kissing a kind princess heal one's crush
And cure bad skin from a broken heart's mush?

41. Love's Diamond

In a cave, hidden shines a rough diamond;
Miners, its potential anomaly
Gauge, clasp rock firmly, as a wedding bond.
Love can lead to sweet lust implicitly
As crystals become diamonds illicit,
Precious and rare in their inequity.
Shall crude passion from your form elicit
Mining fever, greed in fervent piety?
A glittering bauble without foible,
Deserving worship as corollary,
Pursuing you is worth all the trouble;
Heart pumps hot blood from a coronary.
A diamond shined is love extroverted,
A sheltered crystal, love introverted.

42. IT Girls

Data travels quick with information,
At the speed of light with technology;
Global village in communication,
Magical, complex as biology.
Human with machine interact at work;
Who is smarter, human or computer?
Perhaps, both operate in this network:
Nervous system=wires and brain=hard-drive per
Company. Each must learn this new language,
Spoken well by the savoir-faire elite.
The light of the cave has tamed the savage;
Reboot our brains with 'Control Alt Delete'.
Somewhere, pretty girls are mathematic;
They stun, though their bodies are dielectric.

43. Christian Empress

Her very air speaks of magniloquence;
She stirs lofty feelings ineffable --
Ordinary people boast eloquence
In her company. She is affable
To visitors, though I but speculate
Her conversations. Her manners bequeath
Upon visitors – class, I calculate,
But retain humanity underneath.
I must confess that I am so impressed
The history of Anglicanism,
Future, belong to this Christian Empress.
Perhaps she'll avert the cataclysm
Revelations foretold this Anglican?
With understanding and wisdom, she can!

44. Hope From The Pope

The cheering crowd shall hail,"Long live the Pope!
Whose travels and celebrations enshrine
God's Kingdom in glory, power and hope!"
The Holy Vatican and Sistine shine,
Blessing communion with a holy grail.
Italy's honour, Roman oracle
From a foreign land, may he never fail
To lift Lord and people from debacle
And ruin! Pious Christian dictator,
Worthy title, Holy Excellency,
Strong may he lead, voluble orator
Of God-inspired Word and pure decency.
How to appease dear God for Man's falling?
Listen and learn, heed well God's voice calling.

45. One-Legged Nun

I wonder how moves a lame gad-about
Across a circus on screen? Shall we jape
At her limping struggles or shall we pout?
Watching her act, even now, I do gape,
Awed by her agility, less so lame.
And ethically, is exploitation
Of cripples, worth entertainment and fame?
A one-legged nun, a 'fun' acquisition
Role, with Catholic boys in the altar
Living dangerously in small hick towns...
But curious, confused, we shall not halt her;
Maybe, she'll play it seriously with frowns?
The roles she acts constantly bemuses;
A one-legged nun may simply amuse us.

46. Group Date

A group date: an evening of basketball
Watching tall men throw a ball – how grizzly;
Applauding with the loud, teen crowd enthrall,
At shots, as if amused in this drizzly
City; in defense, jeer at visitor
As our stomachs digest a nice free meal.
When treated by the boss, one cannot bore
One's self with whatever might be more real.
A smooth ride to and fro by limousine,
Courtesy of the nice boss from Chevron.
Amazing, we didn't stop for gasoline,
Considering we lost and Boston won;
We could have been high on fumes as a treat!
Though we held our seats tight, we felt defeat.

47. Artists Loft

Two bright artists in search of their dream loft,
Hoping to lift their poor souls to success;
Wishes and fantasies keep them aloft,
Above their finances, shattered pieces
Keeping them tattered, and yet creative.
How many suffered to be artistic --
Experiences and fantasies festive,
Balance by thoughts, actions more realistic?
Of for that unforgettable painting
Which catapults artists to their zenith,
The one through history, leaves crowds panting;
As on a trapeze, the acrobat, lithe,
Thrills the big, breathless crowd who paid money;
Artists having careers, ain't that funny?

48. Creative Luck

For luck, Aladdin's lamp must be furbished;
Genie grants three wishes in flirtation.
Losers thinks success and wealth are rubbish,
Dreaming, goal-setting but irritation.
To celebrate three dreams we shall party:
Congratulate ourselves, place on display
Our trophies of success; fill our pantry;
Rummage our coloured closets and be gay!
Artists unite for meritocracy,
Full of whims, fables, fripperies, caprice;
The best phantasmic aristocracy --
Free, loose and natural without malice.
Cosmic, universal is this fusion,
Powerful, energetic, the fission!

49. Beauty's Fool

Zelda is a temp clerk in a garage.
Plain, simple and quiet, she does her work
Efficiently. Paid a minimum wage,
She lives month by month with a lazy jerk.
An older man in suit, respectable,
Distinguished, occasionally visits
To socialize and patronize. Able
To command attention, he stands or sits
As he chats with the staff. He smiles, teasing
Them about their skills, duties, competence,
Then exits theatrically. One thing
He did notice – Zelda's lack of pretense.
One day when he said she was "Beautiful
As always", she blushed, not his beauty's fool.

50. Poncho Honcho

On cobbled stones, courtyards, she might hobble
As 'Quasimodo the Hunchback', huffing
As he escaped from cruel crowds trouble.
Heavy smokers with damaged lungs puffing,
Exert extra effort too. Yet, healthy
As she is, I surmise, if she is wise
To pretend so. Why would such a wealthy,
Attractive and charming lady disguise
Herself? Esmeralda was beautiful,
Compassionate; if she wanted a fuss
Or warm our hearts, she need not play the fool!
Acting disabled is an onerous
Decision, like working for a honcho
Who begs for money, wears a torn poncho.

51. Eccentric Priest

Father Leander worshipped a fetish,
An idol of a woman named Hero
Whom he knew from a past life. He did wish
At Mass that he could save an entire row
Of front seats for her entrance in his life.
At night, he would polish the stone statue
Secretly, praying devoutly his wife
Would return! He cried nightly with tissue,
Wiping tears away. "Why did we both drown?
Hellespont was so aptly named Hell's Point!
When will we ever meet again?" A frown
Lined his brow, feeling tired in every joint
As he stretched. He'd never be a male beast
Virile, masculine, thus he was a priest.

52. Humble Will

Actor, playwright and humble suitor Will
Shakespeare, premier poet and English bard,
Suffered for love out of his own free will.
Rhythm and rhyme in every line, though hard,
He penned well. Several plays did he excel
In, to entertain his Queen from a fit.
For Her love, he went through Heaven and Hell,
Yet deserving of Her, he felt unfit.
Great and mighty was his pen for Queen Beth,
Volatile, Tempestuous Titiana!
Loyal and servile was he till Her death;
He honoured his Bess – Long live Brittania!
Passionate of Her, divided by caste,
He loved the Virgin Monarch, glorious, chaste!

53. All Mighty Parents

Alleluia might father, mother,
For nurturing all of us and caring,
Raising us decently. You did smother
To protect us from harm, taught us sharing
And respect within our big family.
Religion and God, we do understand
Through attending school, Church and homily.
Holy Bible and rosary in hand,
We fight the devil, domesticated
By Christianity and education.
Simple, behaved but sophisticated,
We grew glad, took many a vacation
Together, for memories that survive.
We love each other just being alive!

54. Pygmy Philosophy

"God made Man and Woman." says the pygmy,
Welcoming tourists to Eden Island.
"Here all practices, as polygamy
Has its place with races." Adds the fire-brand.
"In Egypt, we built a gold pyramid.
In Babylon, a tower, quixotic
Illogical, it was destroyed amid
Much fuss by God who thought it exotic.
He could not see how a blue mongoloid
Could order around the mute red negroid
Who struck gold with a yellow caucasoid.
'This does not look good.' He thought paranoid.
So, we babble to this day. The Crusades
Though, will unite us into God's Brigades!"

55. History's Paradox

"Racism and prejudice," said kill-joy
"Ferment wars and discontent, a loathsome
But necessary movement to destroy
Inter-breeding and mixing, the flotsam
Of Society." Destroy the effigy
Of the tolerant. It's no mystery
That inequality and synergy
Are a paradox in world history.
To continue in this sport of charades
Of intermingling allows parasites
To feast on great men, colourful parades
Notwithstanding. Civil rights lead to fights,
Rallies separating friend from enemy.
Assassinations end this infamy.

56. Moths To Flames

Moths hover near flames although perilous,
Fascinated as they burn. No stalemate
Zone exists that is safe. Supercilious
Butterflies avoid such a fatal fate
By evading fires and forbidden thoughts.
To pursue wild flowers, depravation,
Though bees sting the curious. In deserts, droughts
Dry shrubs and thirst throats in deprivation.
'All words, no action.' A visionary
Dreams, each denying the other ingrate
His company extraordinary.
Every immigrant might deracinate
From her ancestry. If so, oh pray thee,
That we shall succumb to someone pretty!

57. Domestic Enterprise

Three hundred sixty six days for leap year,
An extra day for the new millennium:
Bravely we shall banish our every fear,
Welcoming adventures to rid tedium
From our lives, like an annual spring cleaning,
With refreshed hearts, we'll continue caring
For loved ones and needy. With our cooking
The famished will be fed. Our housekeeping
Shall be done in our finest livery!
We'll succeed in domestic enterprise,
On-line shopping, door to door delivery.
A housewife's dream, a suburban surprise,
We'll be millionaires in home-based business,
Rewarded, from our slavery, busyness.

58. Victory To Victims

"When will we win?" In pain, wails the plaintiff.
"Wounds cannot heal with thorns. As a victim,
I know. We hide from most evils, scared stiff
For our lives." To live in peace, all vermin
Must be eradicated. They oppressed
People with impunity, criminals
With money and cunning. Many depressed
Humans pray to God with daily hymnals,
Yearning for the day, they ride triumphant,
Free in the streets, their homes. To imprison
And punish, to stomp like an elephant
All cruel criminals without reason,
Then shall victory come to the vanquished!
From God's Kingdom, all evil be banished.

59. Family Prayers

For family, nightly, I pray for health,
Empowering, energizing goodness
For loving and living wisely in wealth
And prosperity. With daily gladness,
I say with grace that even God's Heaven
Could be created right here on Man's earth.
To rise in glory and honour, brethren
We conquer even death! Created dirt,
When purified, we become immortal.
May we exist in ever-lasting peace
Ushered in gay tidings through the portal
Of Paradise! Lives permanently leased,
We owe to our Creator's kind wisdom,
Entry to the Lord's eternal Kingdom!

60. Chicken Gibbet

Fouler than foul, entrails, gut and giblet
Carved out of the poor, frail, love-sick chicken,
Who pining for her love, on a gibbet
Did hang, her foolish heart and neck broken.
Spying one night, she witnessed imbroglio,
Angered by jealousy, her mate's gimmick
To test fidelity, trust. Gigolo
That he was, he drove this poor love-bird sick,
Dancing with some chick in a honky-tonk
Bar. Sadly, this flirtatious dalliance
Upset her; she drank alcohol till zonked.
Motto: 'When bound happy in alliance,
Do not mistrust, nor test love, nor dally,
As some curious cat in a drunk's alley.'

61. Lewd Prude

"To draw or not to draw." A denial
Would be wasteful. It's harmless, vicarious,
As fantasy harms none. A sleep vial
Eases sweet slumber, although precarious
If poison. An artistic portfolio
With nudity is not pornography.
Poems, plays compose a creative folio.
Sketches, paintings are not photography,
Real enough to embarrass as a coward.
Perhaps, if taboo subjects such as sex
Are discussed, written, portrayed, then forward
Moves education in matters that vex.
Do not accuse artists, however lewd,
If progress occurs, salvaging a prude.

62. Braille Braggadocio

Like a woman blinded by love, through braille
I'd imagine reading your face. Request
Me to daily care for you as if frail,
Though wicked passion like a storm tempest
Churns the heavens! A rainbow covenant
After each flood of feelings superior
Engulfs us both. Promise this sycophant
That doubts and criticisms inferior
Shall not part us both, indomitable
Spirit that we share. Let's not facetious
Be, regarding our love formidable!
Great and mighty are our tough trapezius
Lifting our true love chiaroscuro;
Truly, this is lusty braggadocio!

63. Meteoric Nights

Poems such as these must love letter-perfect
Be, to enamour and to ingratiate
A suitor such as I, with you. Infect
My aching soul; my body initiate
Into raging fires of indiscretion,
Enflamed with swirling desires meteoric!
Literally, release inhibition,
Which restrains hidden passions terrific,
Consuming our souls! Nights spent industrious,
Delirious in grand ecstasies, foreign
And fulfilling. Oh, a diamond lustrous
Is our love! Immersed in its light, we deign
To face the world. Would I be delinquent
To forego this and enter a convent?

64. Yogi Bearah

Stretching, bending, twisting moves in yoga
At home, saves him the costly excursion
To the East. He'd suit a Roman toga
If he shaved his legs. Demon possession
Gives him nightmares, but watching kids cartoons
Keeps him laughing. At night, he's huggable
As a stuffed bear. We romp like two baboons
In a zoo! He's warm, smart and lovable.
Best of all, he is funny with humour
In him and skilled in essays and drawing.
He's faithful not to leave if a tumor
From cancer grows in me, not withdrawing
From pain. College trained, he should been chef
If he did not attempt recipe theft.

65. Victims Vindication

After assaults, Che had to vindicate
Herself by winning in court, proving right
Justice and Truth do surely indicate
Her innocence. She had to face a fight
In court. Che accused her male attackers
Of sexual assault; they denied their wrong.
Not believing her, the legal workers
Plotted to make her lose. Not being strong
Nor rich, she lost despite the truth! She wrote
Poetry and song hoping success would
Make up. Eventually, the public vote
Went in her favour. Money and fame could
Assuage internal victimization.
She won the battle of vindication!

66. Tit For Tat

Love buffets may lure voracious gourmands,
Feasting gluttons. A finicky gourmet,
Quality over quantity, demands,
Selecting the finest. Many a nay
Prevents complications leading to fights.
Weak wills and weak knees lose to choosy might.
Tit for tat from a lovers spat and spites,
Avoided by discernment, gains one sight.
Perhaps domestic violence, with punches,
Awakes lovers now strangers, pummeling
Each other as enemies. Those hunches
Ignored, if followed, avoids the trampling
Of one's heart. Like a bird in hand to crush
Or free, in love, do choose well or eat mush.

67. Breathing Same Air

Separated by not meeting, a yawn
Sufficed to inhale her air. Feeling trapped
By shyness, Jo took the Joyce bus each dawn
To see her 'crush'. Her love illusions wrapped
Around for a figure. The same space enclosed
Them in the bus, sharing each other's breaths.
If only an accident could expose
Their emotions, as shown by heaving chests
Secretly gasping for air! The unknown
Future looked dim, full of fear and sadness
Without each other. If the hot wind, blown
By escaping lungs released their madness,
Passion would occur with inhalation!
If not, fainting by asphyxiation.

68. Family Lunacy

"Voices in the head, bats in the belfry."
Chita chanted repeatedly clapping,
"Bondage in birth and blood may not go free!"
Family members regret their slapping
Of her cheeks as a child. In the attic,
She subsisted on air, a vegetable
Mentally. Ashamed of their lunatic,
Family banned her eating at table.
The singing and rocking rhythmically
Led to rolling her eyes without control.
Diagnosed possessed, hypnotically
Lost in inner space, her face became droll
Enough for laughter. A sanatorium
Welcomed her although her spirit did fume.

69. Echo Recollection

From girlhood, I recall some memories,
Which I treasure. Will a painful parting
From them wreck my soul's personal stories?
From past lives, loves, I'm not worth a farthing
To in this life, I do dream of England.
Lovely island people, full of power,
Might, do my lost loves come from this far land?
Magnificent Queen, high in a tower,
Have mercy on me, this poor commoner.
Images of romantic royalty,
Echo inside, like a happy summer,
Memorable, intense reality.
Past loves still bring fantastic happiness!
Reincarnation exists, I confess.

70. Sideburns In Suburbia

Clothing casually worn, haberdasher
Nowhere in sight. No parasol nor shawl
To keep one dry and warm. Every cashier
In the suburb mall, charms one with a drawl.
Sideburns and glasses, a drool and dribble,
Just to seem intelligent, sociable,
And voluble enough not to quibble.
Mingling with obese is equitable.
Opposites may attract and co-exist.
Fat and thin watch colour television.
Suburban leisure is seldom sexist.
Men and women both thrive in derision
Over who has the biggest belly – beer
Drinkers or pregnant women who can jeer.

71. Funny Foster Home

Welcome to the fun home for the senile!
Family run, home caring for seniors,
Experienced, trained, without even one vile
Rumour to mar reputation for worse.
Warm meals and snacks prepared for quick nibbling
Satiate one's palate. Violent foster
Home this ain't. We wipe the patients dribbling
Mouths and spills. No crazy roller-coaster
Here, though vomiting occurs. We fritter
Lazy days aided by medication.
We sweep and mop daily, throw out litter
As most houses. Sleeping in sedation
Heals most mental problems with dementia --
Excusable, no more euthanasia.

72. Burger Buns

Popular people chew on hamburger
In a bun, drink cold pop and digest fries.
Hotdogs too satisfy the sharp hunger
Of fans. Many a hot, fast food franchise
Made millionaires, cooking over a grill.
Greasy, cheesy, tasty meals on griddle
Fattened obese gluttons. O, what a thrill
To solve the world's weight problem. A riddle
Causing billions in dieting. Hobnob
With many a fat, friendly, big behind
On some stool, teeth grinning like corn on cob,
Oily as butter. Maybe we can find
Booth seats wide enough for the overrun
Butts? Or munch on burgers without a bun.

73. Desert Gambling

Gambling fever strikes people in desert
Cities – Reno, Vegas. Caution's forfeit
Is the price of risk. Like eating dessert,
Machines gobble coins for human defeat.
How many hope to get rich quick from luck?
Strike oil, jackpot for a desert fortune,
Beats working 9 to 5 for a cheap buck.
Kids play arcade games; moments opportune
For millions, adults stake. Does decadence
Of character follow with each prospect?
Does God bless the lucky with providence?
Some say it's sinful, which gamblers expect.
But many take chances with their money,
For without it, they're full of baloney!

74. Gore Vs. Bush

Wars, akin to campaigns, political,
Strategical, are decided by vote.
Rivals want to lead, diametrical
In personality and thought. Both dote
On their public: one full of blood and gore,
Warrior in suit; the other in a bush,
Saving his skin. Both in speeches can bore.
In action and election, ambush
Surprise win might befall this great country.
Both dream of better, financial futures.
Both hoping to be part of history.
If the country were wounded, their sutures
Would heal it. But who can tell at present
Which one we will eventually resent?

75. Nell In A Shell

Her grandma died leaving her all alone.
No one left to care, in a mountain shack.
Electricity, television, phone --
Not one around. She had many a lack,
Poor girl. It's good it was just a movie.
Long hair washed in lakes, just like a hippie.
A strange language all her own – how groovy,
Without drugs, dumb, alone, full of poesy.
The scientists all thought,"How natural
A girl in the wilds can be spiritual."
Analyzing why she seemed magical,
Despite their psychological ritual.
'Get her out of hell, wild girl in a shell,
Psychoanalyze what's weird about Nell.'.

76. Spic 'N Span

Domesticated women's obsessions
Include: cleaning, arranging furniture,
Cooking meals and polishing possessions.
A professional, not an amateur
Can run homes automated with: vacuum
Cleaner, operate well a clothes washer,
Without staining (or throwing a tantrum),
Dry clothes without burning in a dryer,
Run dishwasher without breaking dishes.
Could those with a pedigree of Spanish
Understand cleaning machines fetishes?
Many maids visit homes, work with relish
'Til the job's done. Possibly, Philippine
Servants can outdo their service and shine.

77. Lady Banshee

Listen to the banshee's high-pitched screeching,
Which in our enthralled hearts, its wailings wrench
A twinge of fear. No amount of preaching
Halts the fascinating charm of the wench.
Lore and myth abound of women, restless,
Disturbed both in life an death. Evening strolls
Alone and soon one's involved in their mess:
Murder, suicide, lost love. Sounds like rough growls
Or loud howls scream these terrifying ghosts,
Restless and tortured for eternity!
Who can heal their suffering? Holy boasts
Could lay to rest their sick souls from pity.
Stop their source of pain and bless their burial
Site with holy water. These blessing heal.

78. Lovers Limericks

Beauty and love to an ignoramus
Are illusions, foreign as iguana,
Elephant, and the hippopotamus.
Maybe a few puffs of marijuana
Might loosen their loving and playful ids?
Relax their inhibitions and prisons
That controlled and repressed them as young kids?
Specially spoken to form liaisons,
Love comes in all dialects, lexicons.
Lovers should shout poetry and climb mountains,
Have fun and limerick as leprechauns!
Knowledge would shower form endless fountains.
Attraction delights enough to elope,
Springing on nimble feet as antelope!

79. Bimbo Cat

Infidelity leads her to propose
Marriage as beginning a new epoch.
She'd wear a white wedding gown and compose
Her own ceremony by a small loch.
Surgery fashionable – lobotomy
Was a success on her, thus she frolics
Merrily with endowed anatomy.
Slurring is sexy by alcoholics,
So she mimics their accents. A maniac,
On stage, with the presence of a diva,
Her nerves jittered, a hypochondriac.
Legend says she was nude as Godiva,
Quite witty in American chit-chat,
Often wishing she were a cool, slick cat.

80. Telepathetic

Out of curiosity, the ouija board
Coerced our fingers to play. Obsession
For information led to questions, bored
Adults soon trapped by its strange possession.
Amazingly, it worked! As telepath,
Moving the glass led to premonition
Of the board's thoughts and words. The aftermath?
I began to move it by volition!
Voices in my head caused me to mutter,
"I am a god in reincarnation!"
This was the summary of the matter.
Then, my family in consternation,
Begged me to forego this weird connection,
Which changed me, and choose their conversation.

81. Puppet Parody

Pinocchio was a wooden boy puppet.
He wanted to be real though transsexual.
The blue fairy granted his wish, strumpet
That she was. His father wanted mutual
Love, since he was a lonely carpenter.
He had carved his handsome, wooden dolly
To keep him company. Not a fakir,
But poor, he rejoiced over his folly,
Wishing his marionette would also crow,
For his future success show to debauched
Folk. The boy was knobbly as a scarecrow
And his nature was endearingly gauche.
Ghepetto trained him to dance in gaudy
Attire, a real cute boy in parody.

82. Shy Pyromaniac

Misunderstanding many a meaning,
Being slightly ill with mythomania,
Queen saw 'Cinderella', in her sibling.
Pitying her poorness, pyromania
In Her blood, Queen burned her castle. Passion
Raged quickly like the Great Fire of London!
She lost her towers of condescension
And helped stop the blaze. Her mask she did don
To hide shyness. Curriculum vitae
Read 'Shy Pyromaniac', as crystal orb
Predicted. The weaver — poor 'Arachne',
In Her sister enviably observed,
So a black widow of 'Dulcinea'
Queen transformed, punishing down millennia.

83. Wicked Wicca

Creative people who practise arts, crafts,
Believe in magic and plenty a spell.
Humour wrinkles their eyes and many laughs
From their bellies shake. However, in hell
Evil witches, wicked warlocks cackle,
As they spitefully poison recipes,
To give one aches and pains. They might shackle
One in dreams to serve them. On precipice,
They dangle one dangerously, causing
Accident, imaginary illness,
Leading to death. Malevolence and sin
Enter cruel hearts even in stillness.
Goodness and holiness but chimera,
Their main goal is end the Christian Era.

84. Cruel Crusades

Holy battles were the Christian Crusades.
God's name in vain, like Jesus on the Cross,
Deluded the masses with these charades.
Innocence and ignorance, both a loss
Replaced with knowledge of Christ. But burning
The beliefs of worshippers of Goddess,
Caused much blood, pain, suffering and mourning.
Oh, each Castle and Church built, each fortress
Protected to honour grand chivalry
Had a price -- each pagan a sacrifice,
Like Jesus the Saviour in Calvary.
What values for spiritual edifice?
Adam and Eve fled the Garden Eden
In shame. Eve burned; Adam nailed to even.

85. Anna And Red King

Long ago, in a far away palace,
Widow and son, on a long ship voyage
Journeyed on a mission to teach. But lass
Anna was, she felt enslaved in bondage
To a red Asian king, polygamous,
Tyrannous, to monogamous – shady.
She was intelligent. He was famous
And he had a court fit for this lady.
Having vision, he hired this nice teacher,
Old-fashioned though he was. With obedience,
She taught his children, but showed their picture
Map of Siam as false. In allegiance,
They rebuked her, being a foreigner
To royal children, and a commoner.

86. Windows and Gates

The millennium countdown passed 'uno, dos,
Tres'. Y2K did not damage systems
As predicted. Computers run Windows
2000 today – the branches and stems
Of wire networks planted by Mister Gates.
Dropped out of college to design programs,
He stayed home alone years avoiding dates.
For text info, he composed diagrams,
Graphics and charts. He marketed billions
Of softwares for public information.
His dominion over many minions
Has changed the world to Microsoft nation!
All that data valued in megabytes,
He is a genius with a brain that bites.

87. Peaches and Cream

Last night, I awakened to a find dream,
Visiting a souvenir shop in travel.
A pretty girl, skin of peaches and cream
Came close enough, my heart to unravel.
Wholesome and plump, delicious as a fruit.
She leaned, smiling warm to plant me a kiss
On my left pink cheek. Did my sad soul suit
Maddening kindness from the sweetest miss
In this strange Canadian town? At her feet,
I lay my heart, desiring to just squeeze
Her tightly! Blushing cheeks burn in such heat,
Churning volcano erupting in breeze!
Gasping for air, hungry for pink peaches,
Tired eyes shut, longing for what she teaches...

88. E-Romance

The world is now conveniently online,
Reaching reality to cyberia.
Friendships and love are found, all without wine
Nor bread. No need to fear gonorrhea
And syphilis viruses with this chat.
A long distance romance is a low risk
Experience. Conversation stores in FAT
Segments of the precious, writable disk.
Some lured by its novelty, take a chance
On intimacy with unknown strangers.
People who do not get a second glance,
Flirt hours, indifferent to its dangers.
It takes bravery to set a meeting date.
But who knows, one might just find a soul mate!

89. Foreign Zealot

Longing for someone unknown overseas,
Seen in a photo, tourist souvenir
Or movie screen — analyze why this is:
A stranger has a familiar veneer,
Is magnetic as a cool demagogue,
And is possibly unsympathetic
To one's curiosity, as a damn rogue;
If not liked back, one becomes pathetic
And depressed. Oh, if only God would bless
With mutual admiration, each zealot
Fan who loses her sanity, obsessed
With meeting stars, feeling as an idiot.
Preparing for years to see her idol,
She clings to dream with her favourite doll.

90. Expo '86

Excitement grew until Exhibition!
A skytrain instead of a ferris wheel
To ride. Releasing one's inhibition,
Encouraged discovery with new zeal.
Nothing to scream for or lose one's tonsils,
But each citizen became hillbilly,
Seeing the city anew. No fossils
History, nor rockets to be silly
About. Citizen to cosmopolite
Instantly. No unusual cockatrice
To shock one. Nothing rude nor impolite
For embarrassment. Friendly trysts
Perhaps in beautiful, young Vancouver!
To move here would be a wise maneuver.

91. European Journey

Riding the airplane to start, then Eurail
And bus completed itinerary.
Seeing Europe in two months without sail
(To Columbus, Magellan – ordinary).
Surprisingly, the locals were friendly!
Summer, being peak season, had tourists
Crawling like ants. Fashion was so trendy.
Shopping sprees were common, hard to resist.
We saw London, Paris – famous cities,
And Madrid, Vienna, Rome – historical
Sites, beaches, museums and galleries.
We were so eager and hysterical --
U.K. France, Germany, Portugal, Spain,
Greece, Italy, Belgium – it was insane!

92. Heathen In Eden

Civilization with its modern clothes,
Laws and order had formed their mild natures
For centuries. Burdened by many loads
Of embarrassment from legislatures,
Some declared,"Let us shed our second skin.
God created us without this clothing.
All these laws imprison and prevent sin.
Look at our hidden bodies with loathing."
They bought property far off the highway,
Bringing their families to seclusion.
Gradually they paraded in a way
They felt comfortable in collusion.
Primitive people becoming heathen,
Pretending their late return to Eden.

93. Vegetarian Egalitarian

In Chapter 1: 29 Genesis,
God gave Man to eat for food, every plant
Yielding seed. Then Man became nemesis
Of every animal, (seen in a hunt)
As Chapter 9 verse 2. In the Great Flood,
Noah offered animal burnt offerings
To please the Lord; he shed their trusting blood,
Ignored all the poor creatures sufferings.
The Lord said there would be a reckoning
For any flesh eaten with lifeblood shed.
Human and beast heeding this beckoning
Had to avoid eating beings that bled.
Thus, it's better to be vegetarian
Because weighed out, it's egalitarian.

95. Gas Man

Modern vehicles run on gasoline.
Modern humans run on snacks and candy,
When prices drop, many form a long line,
As for a store with sale clothes for dandy
Fashion. The gas man works hard past midnight:
Guarding from robbers, cleaning, counting cash,
Stocking shelves, preventing a violent fight
From happening. Some customers may wash
In the washroom. Some do not pay and run.
Other need company. If their auto
Needs repair, a mechanic has his fun.
To do their best is the station's motto.
Also, to be your neighbourhood town pump.
So be faithful, this station do not dump.

95. Muscle Women

Sweating to build muscles without steroids,
We lift children, seniors, groceries, weights,
Straining and breaking backs (that hemorrhoids
Might ache). Fat is a disease in the States;
Food is good. Yet, a strong nation needs strong
People, therefore we diet, do workouts.
Summers, our goal is to wear a 'sarong',
Skirt or shorts. Occupational burnouts
Are common in medicare. Aerobics
Build stamina and patience. Minerals
Improve our bodies vital statistics.
Miss Universe is perfect. Chemicals,
Radiation, surgery – with vitamins
Are avoided. With faith, prevention wins!

96. Fanatic Crowd

Rushing to touch their star, crowds go amok,
Whooping, hollering, full of malarkey,
Hearts on fire! Elated, they cause havoc
To barriers preventing them. This blarney
Is serious and thrives on their keen delight
To see and touch their magical heroine,
Who epitomizes success. Highlight
Her shining career, with their dreams, on screen.
Celebrities create mass illusion.
Palpitating hearts, minds, mark a heart throb.
She loses rare privacy, seclusion
At the insistence of her eager mob.
In summary, a star makes crowds woozy
With happiness, high on their drug, dizzy!

97. Fave Things

Decorations, toys, gifts, things we all crave
Seen in stores, desired and bought. Favorite
Things are chosen by the degree we rave
Over them. What makes a thing a big hit?
Best of lot? Quality of creation?
The cheapest deal that appeals? Or unique
Items – one-of-a-kind? Satisfaction
Guaranteed, and with the right sales technique,
Fad products are manufactured. With skill,
Customers purchase their lovely treasures,
Thinking a precious, not run-of-the-mill
Thing is in their possession. The pressures
And stress to own delightful things we buy
Off the shelves, with or without them, we sigh.

98. Art & Community

Citizens revolt against elitist
Attitudes in art. Members of public
Associations ask aid from artist
Groups, as politicians from republic
Societies. Unions do cooperate
In organization with awareness
Of the meaning. Art movements operate
With energy, action, belief. Impress
The citizens of Surrey, a suburb
Of various cultures. Experimental
And conventional, movements with the nerve
Of rural, urban, environmental
And commercial. Art and community
Involvement can build both town and city.

99. Copy Cat

Emulating heroines, facsimiles
Of original idols, we copy
Those we admire. Malleable, young pussies
Grow into big cats. Avoid entropy
And decay by example, mimicry
Of energetic leaders we follow.
Personality shadows puppetry,
At times controlled, strings pulled, with heads hollow.
Intimacy with who follows so close,
Rewards one, like an identical twin,
Who shares one's face as mirror. If they chose,
Twins can interchange in life – every win
Becomes two. Mirroring shows one besot
With someone original, cool or hot.

100. Minorities Dilemma

If part of the mainstream majority,
Fair and easy decisions are voted,
To make rules for all. But minority
Groups, who are small, different, have noted
Their lifestyles and selves are alternative,
Which makes them realize being different
Means being outcast, not being native,
As the general populace. Abhorrent
As it seems, they are not degenerate,
Nor contrary to public opinion.
Although, they might differ or separate
From majority rules, a desertion
Is inhumane, against democracy.
As well, revolutions would be crazy.

101. Good-Bye Muses

Our spirits cannot bridge the large crevasse
That splits us opposed thus, separation.
What bound us to our willing chains, alas
No longer does. Now incarceration
Ends and we are 'incommunicado'
Again, silent, unknown, as if nothing
Awakened us once to each other. Do
Muses, Bard, in union have anything
In common, after what once could inspire,
Poetry, is no more? Each poem immortal,
A tribute to both, though the fates conspire
Against us! Conscious of our old mortal
Selves, death is the last good-bye, my Muses,
With arguments, separations, ruses...

102. Vegetarian Science

Studying women's teeth, note herbivores
Have flat molars, no fangs. A herbalist
Grows plants for their health, not for carnivores.
Shopping wisely for a grocery list,
Fill it with a wide variety of fruit,
Milk, green leaf, grain, seed, nut and vegetable.
(Whether we become cows or goats is moot.)
Daily servings with meals on the table
Improves health and energy — a science
In diet. Vegetarians eat herbal
Plants, read books on occult, New Age, séance,
And trace family ancestry to tribal
Clans and dinosaurs who ate leafy plants,
Like the brontosauri eaten in hunts.

103. Ugly Photos

If part of the mainstream majority,
Fair and easy decisions are voted,
To make rules for all. But minority
Groups, who are small, different, have noted
Their lifestyles and selves are alternative,
Which makes them realize being different
Means being outcast, not being native,
As the general populace. Abhorrent
As it seems, they are not degenerate,
Nor contrary to public opinion.
Although, they might differ or separate
From majority rules, a desertion
Is inhumane, against democracy.
As well, revolutions would be crazy.

104. Cocaine Insanity

Divorces do cause a great disturbance
In family relations. The ruins
That remain are not worth the remembrance;
All are losers, no one in this war wins.
Taking drugs to escape, no diversion
Is worth ensuing addictive problems.
With personal or social perversion
Complicating issues, the grim emblems
Of drug abuse worsens: marks from needles,
Viruses, loss of stamina, comas
One never awakens from, or wheedles
For deadly drugs causing hematomas.
Why experiment with fatal cocaine
When family problems drive one insane?

105. Bawdy Lair

Poet, whose name means 'den of prostitute'.
Read by an American star with flair,
Who wears Armani suits not destitute.
How fortunate you are to so ensnare
Such a fine woman! Did you offer hash
In essay form, translated from the French
Original? Did you prepare and wash
Your wispy, white hair to entice the wench?
Or did you order 'flowers of evil'
To be delivered to her home doorstep
On her birthday? Failing, would she snivel
At your lack of memory and accept
Defeat at your cruelty, Baudelaire?
Nay, she's not a whore for your bawdy lair!

106. Bacon & Ham

What's a popular order for breakfast?
Cornflakes & milk, eggs with bacon & ham,
Pancakes & toast, fried rice & sausage, last
But not least, served in bed at Buckingham
Palace. A servant checks morning e-mail,
Hands them on a platter. Queen at repast,
Gets tons of letters daily without fail.
Loyal monarchists, young & old, quite fast
Contact her on-line. At old Sandringham
House, she just might prefer a quick, light switch
For lunch or a snack, a nice sandwich – spam
With lettuce and tomato. She's bewitched
By articles of her in newspaper,
And family in some royal caper.

107. Spanish Stumble

News groups gossiped of a royal stumble.
Queen of Spain had tripped, then was assisted
By U.S. President without grumble.
The First Lady looking on, resisted
Helping, not understanding the Spanish
Courtesy, its customs, language, nor pride,
Being American. Who can say which
Reason? Maybe, she alone could decide
Whether helping a lady is polite
Or not? Since royalty in the White House
Is irony — Democracy won the fight
Over Monarchy. But her gallant spouse
Was kind enough to allow the visit.
Anyway, maybe Spain's Queen was unfit?

108. Venus Flytrap

A beautiful plant that catches insects,
Native American, Venus Flytrap
Grows by eating creatures one disinfects.
A movie star drinks her fanatics sap
For energy. If caught in deshabille,
Within her trailer, when paying visit
To her set, her trap doors shut fast at will,
Preventing one a glimpse to solicit
Attention, an autograph. Who knows why
We hover as pests: hungry as a wasp,
Buzzing bee, dirty fly, or butterfly
Flirting, yearning, unafraid of her grasp?
Yes, I would play an insect imposter,
To meet a star in order to toast her!

109. Suburban Doldrums

Home offices can help depopulate
Stuffed, urban companies in skyscrapers.
A suburban job shift does segregate
Ship liners from the canoes. Newspapers
Covering city life, now read on schedule
With breakfast, allowing the new freedom
To read each article. For every fool
Who quits pressure jobs, suburban boredom
Rewards with a variety of duties:
Enjoying the paper, doing laundry,
Watching tv (ogling all the beauties),
Cooking and cleaning (sure beats the foundry),
Filing and organizing in doldrums,
Surfing, chatting and e-mailing the bums.

110. Neuphoria Club

All fashionably gay people with wax
Faces, noses in the air, frivolous,
Flirtatious, bored with the anti-climax
Frequent the swanky club. So melodious
Are the tunes, that weird megalomania
Fills the atmosphere. A pandemonium
Of bodies sway in rhythm, miasma
Of sweat. Stars visit this harum-scarum,
Mingling with worshippers in a hot dance,
As if elated by a stimulant;
Hypnotic and magnetic is the trance,
Psychotics to an anti-depressant.
Falling in love is one high euphoria,
Insanity, meeting stars, dei gloria.

111. Ballyhoo

Scary horror picture shows that go 'boo',
Full of fake blood, scripts of hyperbole,
Exaggerated as sneezing 'achoo',
Or nachos with extra guacamole.
All are entertaining as naïve youth.
We throng theaters to see: hip, young tomboys,
With girls next door, anxious and still uncouth,
The stage before growing up, liking boys,
When it still mattered to be 'hot' or 'cool',
'In'; phase where a boy becomes man, mere lad
Inexperienced, but a young, simple fool.
Many believe advertising – the fad,
Ignorant of the subconscious hidden,
Then growing up, realize they're just kiddin'...

112. Hollywood Establishment

"Lights, camera, action!" routine studio
Script, requiring technical discipline,
Professionals of movie and video,
Experts producing films of virtue, sin.
Directors, producers, influential
In the background, manipulate media
For the masses. They must maintain cordial
Relations with staff. Encyclopedia
Minds develop scenes, as a connoisseur
Of wines with alcohol. Escapism
Allows actors to role-play, from hauteur
To humility. With realism
They act – billion dollar establishment,
Factory manufacturing figment...

113. Feminism Herstory

Women through centuries: from the farmyard,
Helped men cultivate land, raise family,
Domesticate livestock, till the backyard
For food and survival. The simile
Of men and women extends from: social --
Society's progress, to economic --
Financing budget, to political --
Laws governing all. Old gastronomic
Reasons, women were cooks – switch of careers,
And now women control the arguments
Of equality. Men, much in arrears,
Must give women chances, in documents,
Approved bills, that assertive feminists
Are men's equals, without misogynists.

114. Haunting House

A stranger came with his dead wife's features,
Hundreds of years after her death. Creepy
Premonition was the cruel creatures
Were visitors, come to bring her, weepy
Waif of a wife, in reincarnation.
The ad – a study in psychology,
Lured her who cared with daughter's devotion,
For her mother, now dead. Sociology
Analyzed her a loner, fathomless,
Sensitive, attractive to poltergeists.
Without her, the house was all emptiness,
Dead children, no heirs. 'Is it her disguised
As another woman? Strange, how haunting
Her small face was when murdered by hanging'

115. Hyperbolic Lecturer

Impatient with students, he'd execrate
Aloud,"Damn this ESL class! Diction
And Grammar of immigrants desecrate
The English language." His erudition
Angered, but he'd say,"To err is human"
Forgiving their ignorance. Cockiest
Around pretty girls, he strutted – a man
Whose motto,'Errare humanum est'
Made him popular with intellectuals
Who pitied those less blessed. Intelligence
Caused his exaggeration. Class rituals
Involved criticizing his rapt audience.
Professor Wroth performed perfunctory
English lectures that were exemplary.

116. Grunge Gal Pals

Pre-puberty when gals were quite grungy,
Wild and free like boys, a tomboys heyday:
Two biked, ran, skated, and jumped the bungee,
Just like the male gender. At any day
Of the week, common attire: jean jackets,
Jeans and t-shirts. Believing in kismet,
The two gals loved each other, had lockets
On, traded photos, as a calumet
Pipe seals close friendship. Between both a clique,
Special meanings, promises not to blab
About each other's dreams, feelings. Unique
Secrets they kept: how much of their thighs flab,
And tummies jiggle, what size of brassiere
Each wears, how wide a wiggle their derrieres...

117. Crumpled Paper

In the first place, it was all fictitious:
The admiration, the embroidery
Of emotions felt, keeping gratuitous
Photos and mementoes of ornery
Stars, who loved only themselves. Expedite
Healing by crushing photos of frou-frou
Types – glamorous egotists. No respite
Unless one does this, flushing down the loo,
Wastes that make one ill. Maybe a ceasefire
Might have worked. It hurt to be so callous,
Throwing treasured souvenirs. You require
I obey your whims, though I felt envious
Of your beauty. Now I feel aversion.
May my heart too, undergo conversion.

118. Coffee Morning

Wake up, change, brew coffee in the morning.
Get your gears going, wired-up on coffee.
It's the routine shared by workers, boring
But so functional. Only a small fee
For the caffeine high. Dirty dishes, sink
Piled up, re-use, recycling and garbage
Dealt with. (Unending cycles make one think
Of immortality. Poets verbiage
May have some truth.) A brief, cleansing shower
Wakes one's body, rousing the mind and nerves
Alone is foolish. Holistic power
Operates better, avoids lethal swerves
From routine, basis of a functional
House, office, factory and hospital.

119. Badminton In Baguio

As children, we were elves living mountain
High in a town of famed rice terraces,
Where natives with Americans attain
Fun, harmony and contentment. Bases,
Parks, golf courses brought locals happiness.
We rode horses and go-carts with laughter!
One family, friendly neighborliness
And living happily ever after...
All summer long: volleyball, badminton,
Warball games, playing in our loved garden.
We had so much fun, we cared not who won.
All were smiling, children, men and women!
Fondly, we remember life in Baguio.
I'd stage it again as impresario.

120. Tempestuous Temp

A storm can churn the seas, shifty tempest,
Tossing boats to and fro. Temporary
Limbo when someone quits, positions best
Filled by temp agencies. Coronary
Attack of panic, but a variety
Of temps available for offices
Fill the positions notoriety.
Brief training, then the short break for recess,
Fill the temps mornings. Any moodiness
Soon vanished with time. A nice skillful
Worker decides to stay from the goodness
Of her heart. She needs money and a dull
Routine to pay her monthly bills. Whether
She survives the storm depends on weather.

121. Holy Rood

A holy man sentenced to die by cross
His love revolution to crucify,
Leading us to Heaven, out of Earth's dross.
His healing powers and love sanctify
Us to care for each other, our Jesus.
His virgin pure Mother from Nazareth,
Visited by Holy Spirit. Great news
It was to Mary and Elizabeth!
King David's heir, Joseph a carpenter
Built wood houses and furniture with nails.
He was a good husband, not a hunter.
Their blessed Son's life ended in travails.
Christ's followers increased this millennium.
He will one day triumph in God's stadium!

122. Seconds In Love And Out

Attraction can happen in a second.
An instant high, sigh, and infatuation
Grips your soul, imagination beyond
Reason, reality. Then, frustration
Comes from dissatisfaction with strangers.
Seconds in love, seconds out, in a glimpse
One weighs all opportunities, dangers
And either leaps allured or stays, as wimps
Do, safe but whimpering at a lost chance
At friendship, romance. Instability
Is unhealthy, yet many a romance
Thrives on shifting sands! Liability
For the consequences of excitement
Would maybe guarantee such enticement?

123. Ewe

Peaceful, docile, good Queen Bess faithful sheep
Wander far, as soft clouds on earth that bleat
Insomniacs count many of them to sleep.
Gladly, her queendom rules beyond defeat.
Spreading peace and harmony. Each corgi,
The Queen's pets, jumps for joy, gleefully barks
At their mistress arrivals. At home, she
Sings and laughs. Every public servant harks
Her vibrant voice. Political meetings
With great leaders have followers who flock
To listen to her wisdom. Gay tidings
And resolutions are possibly mocked,
But she handles problems as royalty.
Therefore, she deserves our meek loyalty.

124. Court Her

The old-fashioned ways of the courtesan
Entertaining guests, as with the courtier
Who as suitor in love, an artisan
Are appropriate in pursuit of her.
Weeks, months of wanting her in misery,
Showing her our sick souls pining away
From love of her. Is it a mystery
That she rules our lives? She has her suave way
Of speaking, listening, accepting gifts.
Enamoured suitors don't try her patience.
Courtship is quite acceptable in shifts.
From dawn to dusk, waiting like love patients
For our wonder doctor with persistence.
She heals us all well, through her existence.

125. Titanic Heroin

It was built to impress, the Titanic.
But struck by iceberg, it was swim or sink.
Addicts under influence satanic,
Name their drugs likewise. In a fatal wink,
They live or die at the mercy of drugs
Because they had problems, a pain killer
They sought. When it kills them, society shrugs
Unable to help because the healer
Is a murderer. The victims despair
Is a cry for help. It will be useless
If one hears it too late. Thus, one must care
Society, family. Let's do the best
To defeat killer-drugs such as heroin
If one succeeds, one is a heroine!

126. Hungry Bear

For food and drink, a bear is a glutton
If starving and famished. When one does spoil
Him by feeding him, his pants top button
Has to be undone. 'Food rewards for toil.'
That is his motto. He studied cooking
In college, worked restaurants where obese
People were fed the 'chicken a la king'.
Customers who ate, he could charm and tease.
They tipped him so well, he would often greet
Them like family. Never miss a meal
He's prepared or he will turn on the heat.
Hospitality, food service are real
Meal presentations – art for appetite!
He is both gourmet and gourmand alright.

127. Bitches On Beaches

Brown is beautiful on sunny beaches.
Women, men, children suntan on hot sand,
Hoping to bronze skin, orange as peaches.
If one needs lotion on one's back, some hand
The bottle over, some spread. To compete
In beauty, popularity – body
Consciousness and shape decide. Do replete
Skin, drink liquids, spread lotion. A study
In human interaction, as a swarm
Of bees to flowers pollen, vacation
Triggers the mating season! Could the warm
Air have caused this hot socialization?
Friends, lovers meet in beaches, where pitches
Of sand, hit rejects faces by bitches.

128. Ethnic City

Cities with several ghettos ethnic,
Diverse enough to speak Esperanto,
With sin regress, or progress with ethic.
Music feeds the soul: many a canto,
Ditty, melody, song and calypso
Have been sung from within. To segregate
Peoples is not worth dollar nor peso.
If all cultures harmonize without hate,
Great symphonies, operas, or ballads
May then develop as daguerreotype
Photos. Mixed greens, tomatos make salads --
Variety, the spice of life. Ethnic hype
Marks a protective man's territory.
His music, don't be derogatory.

129. Grumbleweeds

A free pass for two from a store, a date
To remember – my birthday! Someone tip
Me this treat means something, destined by Fate.
Film on mother-daughter relationship,
Moody mama, like the cute blonde in front.
"Excuse me miss, did you move? You're fickle,
Unfaithful, shifting seats, jobs as your wont.
Last time, we met in a cool club. Tickle
Me pink to see you again. Rave and rant
About this movie chick. For a small town,
She looks alright. Later a restaurant
For dinner would be nice." Sadly, a frown
Creased her nice face and she moved seats grumbling
As if bothered by my verbal fumbling.

130. Clay Feet On Pedestal

Statues of gods, goddesses carved from clay,
Honouring humans placed on pedestal,
Heroes and heroines having their day.
'The higher you climb, the harder you fall.'
A saying warns, from those who criticize
Seeing all aspects, both virtue and fault.
Ostriches, heads under sand, ostracize
Problems. However, zealots form a cult
Though weaknesses exist: Achilles heel,
Samson's hair and Jesus chest. Honesty
Humbles many a flawed person. We kneel
Until marble crumbles and amnesty
Granted to us, who worship a hero.
The Roman Empire burned under Nero.

131. Crows In Counsel

Criminal court, men wearing gowns in black,
Dressed up as steel-eyed ravens, donning wigs
Perch on high, judging each evil attack
On Good Society. Evidence as twigs,
Gathered till enough make prosecution
Probable, or else, costly civil suits
Have to be filed. Common prostitution,
Murder, rape, assault, burglary are roots
Of evil, which darken lives, black as crows.
Penalties are meted out by a Judge.
Compensation to victims on escrows
Until the verdict's read. If a big smudge
Taints good people's reputations, Counsel
Might advise the press not to kiss and tell.

132. Healthy Canajuns

Natives, Europeans, in Canada
Explore, exercise and diet. Healthy
Minds and bodies are molded, la-di-da
For West Coast living and looking wealthy.
Health Canada helps aboriginals
Maintain health and fitness in some treaty.
Although natives were the originals
Of this land, they didn't start this committee
Promoting health. A photo of the Queen
With a big grin shows off her nice dental
Work. It hangs in the bright board room wherein
Staff convene for programs: from medical
To dental, vaccinations, diseases,
Plagues, viruses... The fight never ceases!

133. Star's Idiosyncrasy

Odd rumours of her idiosyncrasy
For gossip abounded. Her rejection
Of news 'truths' led to this apostasy.
She started her own press – an injection
Of herself as she saw fit. No contact
With mainstream media or their approval,
Her movies played according to contract,
With no prior screenings. Her removal
Of trust for third party or visitor
Opinions led to many self-writings
On-line. She was both subject, editor
And writer, wary of any writhings
For public attention. For prominence,
She never criticized her eminence.

134. Joe Jacamar

Bright, multi-coloured bird, the jacamar
Insectivorous, from a tropical
Land. If I become insect for a star,
Will you eat me for a meal, typical
Lunch in a dense jungle, my narcissus?
When you dress for an outing, thick pomade
In hair, I forget my pretty muses
For awhile, hand-in-hand to promenade
With you. To celebrate joys of Easter,
Colourful shirts, as feathers of parrots,
Would adorn us, bright enough to give cheer!
Parading our love, gaudy as harlots
Who smoke, or stars who traipse through 'Kookooroo',
We could outshine the queen in Timbuktu.

135. Matron Patron

In promotion of arts, royalty aids
Starving artists for: a cultured event,
Fundraiser, party, charity for AIDS.
To prepare for celebrating Advent,
And Christmas, the generous large expense
Of entertainment with honorarium
Is paid as a much needed recompense.
To create a superb opus magnum,
Lovers of art and culture can endorse
Artists, as powerful entrepreneurs.
Much better than betting on a race horse.
The risks taken on artists works ensures
Prosperity and fame for the matron,
Posterity and wealth for the patron.

136. Nasty Nickelodeon

Red light district in city – a cheap thrill
To peek at women without clothes, porno
In other words. A woman with no frill
Is quite odd, as white keys in a piano,
No black for contrast. Or the tribal hoax --
'Tasadays' naked, wild... A hobgoblin
Feeling it happens on Wreck Beach. They coax
Watchers to gawk and grin, as a gremlin
Causing mischief. Maybe, the kind warden
Will save them from foolishness? The bailiff
Too, might cage them up in his cold steel den.
Having power on them, he gets a whiff
Of sadism, asks,"Your nickelodeon
Performances are they worth your freedom?"

137. No Smoking

After much research, the regulation
Was passed for health. Since the Queen does not smoke
Commonwealth must obey. Segregation
Would be harder. Once popular as Coke,
Cigarettes were found to destroy the lungs
Important for our breathing. Lung cancer,
Heart, throat, mouth, possibly also our tongues
Might be affected. Open sores, canker,
Were signs to watch for, ditto a bad cough,
Discoloured fingertips, anemia, phlegm,
Thick mucus in a sore throat, a harsh rough
Voice as well as intermittent ahem.
Tobacco industry falls, as building
Codes accede to the law of 'No Smoking'.

138. Princess Margarine

Butter is made from cows milk, margarine
From vegetables. The Queen has a shadow,
A princess. Their blood is thick as shortening,
Running in regal veins. She does follow
When she's invited to a rendezvous,
Playing her dainty role with each coxcomb,
Stylish, well-mannered, her teased up hairdo
Copied by the crowd. When in Queen Mom's womb,
She vowed to enjoy wealth and pound-foolish,
She was born to shop. The Queen, penny-wise,
Cut her ample allowance to punish
Her taste. When she begged for more, truths or lies
About her budget were asked the Princess,
Like who spends more on clothes? She must confess.

139. Mother Bee

This millennium, Queen Mom turns a hundred,
A century lived as Queen of the hive.
Born 1900, the lightning thundered
When she took first breath! A century thrived
From childhood, on her dreams of a queendom.
She hoped her country would be united
Like in a fairy tale. When she was Mom,
Her daughter fulfilled this – once divided
Lands became one. From a rich industrial
Clan, she attained royalty by marriage.
A prince charming living in a royal
Castle, courted on a horse-drawn carriage.
We must honour our long lasting Monarch;
She rules us with kindness, as matriarch.

140. Rumour Humour

News lie to sell papers, a false rumour
To shock readers. Some say it by slander,
Others write. Stars with senses of humour,
Don't sue. A lizard's a salamander,
So words spoken and written is libel.
How to damage someone's reputation?
Stars who do not shop for name brands, label
Them cheap, unchic. If seen in a station,
Report they are cruising someone sordid:
A gas attendant, mechanic or thief!
White with blue collar leads to those torrid
Affairs and adultery can bring grief.
Seen with the same gender, he's a homo,
And with a maid, he's a 'major domo'.

141. The Seven Suzara

Once seven dwarves, a smart prince, and Snow White
Lived in a mansion. Each dwarf had one skill,
As they grew up in White Plains, without height.
They were happy, high up on the top hill,
Most wholesome, intelligent, good-looking
And sociable. With their hidden talents
Of art, math, poetry, cooking, healing,
Budgeting, and games, their grateful parents
Gave them everything children could wish for:
Trips to the beach, a mountain home, Sunday
Restaurant lunches, Christmas gifts and lore.
They had loving relatives who could play
All their games. Descending from Caesarea,
They take pride in their blood, the Suzara.

142. Farewell Welfare

Social workers at poverty stare well,
Healthy and detached from the starvation.
Life for the needy waves a sad farewell
Without aid. With approval, elation
Relieves each applicant as existence
Becomes more tenable. Integrity
Does not feed nor clothe, but with persistence
One retains decency. Temerity
In asking for shelter, food, from outreach
Drives by poems, paintings and songs on guitar,
Record the experience. Does one beseech
Both the social worker and avatar
For one's life? If so, may a merciful
Kindness enter hearts to help the tearful.

143. Maid & Her Queen

A Queen admired herself, with folderoi
Jewelry round her neck. Cupidity
Was a facet of her, which did annoy
Maid, whom Queen accused of stupidity.
Maid switched Queen's ornaments, as contagion,
With fake ones, pretending to be docile,
As she aided Queen. Queen's faithful legion
Were wanting honours for old wars, senile
As they were. Queen sent Maid to the garret
To fetch and place the Royal Red Garter,
On her thick thigh. It was coloured scarlet
As blood shed in wars. Queen, of the barter
Unaware, went on her way for gelding
Military horses, warriors knighting...

144. Doctor Cosmetic

Failing tests in forensic medicine
And to stop murderers in surgery
Who caused scars, deaths, Doctor from magazine
Models whose faces, forms in symmetry
Impressed, made a switch to doing facelifts.
Opening clinic, she ironed wrinkles
From old foreheads, eye corners, did nose shifts,
Tummy tucks, breast and chin lifts. All crinkles
Were pulled taut with any altered feature.
Those who had an excess, had a decrease
In size. To satisfy her, each creature
Had to look like her, so she did increase
A few. Monsters of Doctor Frankenstein
Believe their cosmetic doctor on-line.

145. Scarey Scars

Mother's battle scars: from a caesarean
Delivery, our youngest brother,
To these cancers lung, breast and ovarean,
Uterus, kidney, and a gall bladder...
She should win a gold medal for bravery!
Surviving all the pain and the trauma,
She's stronger than a warrior from slavery,
Leading family onward without drama.
Sometimes it seems the surgeons are killers,
Out to end her beautiful, devout life.
All that cutting and blood form fake healers
Is horrible, since she's such a good wife.
It's worse than a movie full of horror --
The surgery room, scalpel, and doctor!

146. Silent Lambastes

Gathering choice bits of news for her 'klatsch'
On the Net, side cup of hot 'espresso'
Beside the mouse, she looks at 'list' to match
Wits with posters. This is 'paraiso',
Especially comments about stars 'kitsch'
Roles. She belongs to elite, 'demi-monde'
Of actresses, whom producers give bitch
Roles to, those few women rich men are fond
Of. Confident in her wit, 'raconteur'
That she is, she spins many a fable
About her and others: from her contour,
Style, education, with cards on table
About her life, innocent of silent
'Lambastes' she gets from envious and violent.

147. Marcos Martial Law

A war hero in 1965
Won the tough presidential election
Through wits, cunning and skill. He did survive
World War Two, had vision and direction,
A beauty queen with breeding for a wife,
Three loving children, educated, smart.
They were a model of family life.
For the poor, sick and hungry, they had heart.
"National progress," voiced this orator
"Is possible with a 'New Society';
Thus, martial law." Imposed this dictator:
A six o'clock curfew for sobriety,
Closed clubs, gun control and intolerance
For criminals for victims deliverance…

148. DWA

Domestic Workers Association
(secretly duty with authority)
Supports domestic rights. Legal faction
Formed by generous lawyers, they take pity
On nannies without money. Such cases
Involving: abuse, overtime no pay,
Illegal entry, no work papers, less
Pay than the minimum wage, no free day,
Are reviewed case by case by staff lawyer,
Legal support and volunteer workers,
Who advise the domestics together
In their best interests. Each nanny swears
She can deserve and know her legal rights.
They volunteer. DWA fights!

149. Social Medical Housework

Society's ills, analyzed case studies
Are done by social workers for clients
Learned in colleges, universities.
Nurses and caregivers helping patients
In foster care homes, write their short reports
For each sick, client-patient in a log
Book: noting down incidents, rude retorts,
Activities, routines, a missing cog
In mental processes. Any victim
Undergoes physical, mental rehab
With these wonder workers, who with great vim
And vigor, lighten up residents drab
Lives. Please take courses in sociology,
Medicine, housekeeping, psychology.

150. Actress Or Queen?

Two choices: a famous movie actress
Or an adroit, popular, royal queen
For a poetess male character's mistress.
Picture the present love triangle scene.
Both are attractive, rich, intelligent.
One makes movies, plays many roles and scenes,
Riveting, versatile for the poem's gent.
The queen, experienced politician, weans
Presidents on the milk of her wise charms.
She has prudence and vast jurisdiction
Over the world: peoples, nations, lands, farms.
All three see their careers with conviction.
As for love, marriage, a relationship?
All would willingly jump on board the ship.

151. Prayer For Pregnancy

O Goddess Earth, grant me a pregnancy
To bless me under laws of chancery
With a daughter, full of obstinacy
As I am. Magic, witchcraft, sorcery
And Christianity – whatever may work
To reward me with a mirror. Female
Power, beauty, and intelligence lurk
Within her since my strange life, I bewail
For any failing or harm that befell
Me and my family. May she avenge
Wrongs done to me, until Heaven and Hell
Comes. May she win battles I lost! Revenge
Shall be within her grasp and great success
Sweet! For I am defeated, I confess...

152. Hoity-Toity

Early morn, hair puffed up in pompadour
Array, so arranged it looks like trompe l'oeil...
Humming of the night before, troubadour
That you can be. Was she lusciously coy?
Did you pretend to be the nincompoop
She delights in, strutting as your hussy?
Cute and funny as sexy, Betty Boop,
Dressed in a revealing mini, pussy
Purring, like an alley cat love duet.
And you, vastly aroused with hair forelock
Dangling over eye, mincing a minuet
To her melody. Crowing as a cock,
You greet the dawn! Losing timidity,
You both enjoy acting hoity-toity...

153. Tarot Truths

Amazing, all three spreads seemed accurate.
The queen, actress, fiance – it was eerie
How the old tarot cards described a fate
With each person, when posed the same query.
A grain of salt taken with the occult
To be safe. Major changes with Tower,
Predicted with the actress, difficult
Litigation, as with the queen. Power,
Fortune Wheel and queerly with queen, falling
In love? Immaturity with Hermit
Indicated too. A Hang Man calling
Sacrifice for growth. The Lovers commit
To love and two cups with fiance. Justice
Served, Temperance, when friends and lovers kiss…

154. Cowabunga

Bored out of her mind, while smoking ganja,
She took a nap and dreamed of koala
Bears eating honey ("miel"), hopping kanga
Roos, way down south in Sydney, Australia.
Equipped with powerful binoculars,
She drove to get a look closer on jeep.
Astounded by the wild particulars,
In the tall, brush grass, she hopped out to peep.
Shocked, "Why, there's a naked man in that bush!
Got to show this to the gals." Camera
In hand, she knelt to take shots of the tush
In bush. Pleased, she drove back to Canberra,
To show her safari, by polaroid
Shots of the attractive, wild Australoid.

155. Coo-Coo Bird

Cooing loudly, the house bird laid an egg,
Proud it finally became a mother.
Round her cage, she paraded lifting leg
To scratch her cocky head, and preen feather.
Our family happily pointed it out,
Feeding bird food, bread, fruit and fresh water,
Rewarding it with sweet praises to shout,
Until,"Hey I think she laid another!"
My nephew screamed. We were again surprised
By this and taking a look, saw the truth.
"How on Earth can she do this?" Sis surmised,
"All by herself in a cage. It's a moot
Chance that they will hatch right with no father!
It takes two birds to hatch eggs together."

156. Salome Saigon

"She dances so well." said old King Herod
"She could have anything she wants!" "The head
Of John the Baptist. For baptism, God
That he denied to me, I want him dead."
Salome replied. "Done." Her sick wish granted,
As St. John's poor head was served by platter.
Centuries later, in Saigon, hated
Foreign city where prostitutes flatter
Soldiers and tourists, sultry Miss Saigon
Enamoured an American soldier.
He remembered her from days now by-gone.
Not having a big chip on his shoulder,
This John, who now wanted to keep his head,
Decided he would take Salome to bed...

157. Squeaky Bed

Horrible how one night, I heard freaky
Noises coming from the bed. A nightmare
To ponder supernatural, squeaky
Pounding, as if possession to beware.
Could it be the horrifying beast sounds
Were coming from ghost demon dogs howling
For release? The nerve-wracking, hellish hounds
That haunt insomniacs with insane growling
From the dead? Invisible, yet the pants
Of the salivating wolf, with huffing
And puffing, I did hear, complete with grunts!
I punched the soft pillow, full of stuffing,
Thinking I could save some poor helpless cow,
Being devoured like an edible sow.

158. MacDonna

Named for someone with maternal instinct
She entertained young crowds as a singer.
Her face and personality distinct
From the rest, her body a harbinger
For sexy women, full of emotion.
Ambitious, capricious, a material
Girl, who set pop music charts in motion!
Outwardly fake, inwardly wishing real
Men would see her. Her career a flip-flop
Roller-coaster ride, dressed as a floozy.
Her movies over-dressed to stay on top.
Some men tripped over her feeling woozy.
She was their star, mistress, prima donna
Special – MacDonalds set's belladonna.

159. Sir Womanizer

That he lied was worse than adultery,
Which was scandalous. Being a braggart,
The public thought it was all flattery,
To have a leader lie with each sweetheart.
He served his terms with lots of confidence,
Epitomizing the nation's big, strong
Ideal. Unfortunately, evidence
And testimony proved his words all wrong.
A mockery of God's democracy,
He served only himself, once crowd pleaser.
In history, he left a legacy
Of immorality, a real teaser.
Proposition 22 to this sir
Leads to adultery, this womanizer!

160. Fil-Veterans

It was World War 2, Manila flashbacks
1942 to 5, a big fight
Because of the Japanese air attacks,
Bombing the city. Citizens took flight
To survive. 'Lolos', 'lolas' remember
The vicious enemies. They reminisce
On sick cruelty and senseless murder
Of Filipinos. Soldiers didn't remiss
Their duties, but defeat monumental,
Without the brave Americans valiant
Efforts to help out for sentimental
Reasons. Removing the bad assailant
Decreed victory to Pearl of Orient,
Freeing Fil-Vets who may now disorient.

161. Grudge Of A Drudge

Faithful as a husband and good father,
Akhbar worked hard supporting family.
They migrated to Canada, farther
Than he dreamed as a boy. He was homely
In childhood but became handsome after
Marriage. Faithful to his wife, he remained
Despite her illness, when no more laughter
Filled their sad lives. Any status they gained
They treasured. Sometimes, he went to dance clubs
Looking for fun until his wife caught him.
"I need to enjoy my life. Drinking pubs,
And bars have energy, vigor and vim!
Preventing me from this, I hold a grudge
Because I'm a healthy man, not a drudge!"

162. Dull House

As a young girl, both kidneys encumbered
By failure, I stayed home to entertain
Myself with a doll house. The world slumbered
On without me, as I made my domain
Of little people. Could be nephritic
Problems that changed me to namby-pamby
Sweet dialogue, from the sharp, cool critic
I could be. Cursed illness from a whammy,
Pinning voodoo dolls, created Grumpy,
Tiny plastic and wood doll, Pugella,
All plastic – my younger brother's frumpy
Piece, when I quit school. Or did flagella
Cause the infection? Sometimes, though drowsy,
I played with little dolls who were frowzy.

163. Gee Cats

Just off White Plains Avenue, on EDSA
Highway, a building servicing autos,
Luxury cars (excluding calesa)
Devotes staff, services, products, mottos
To fixing cars. Computerized service
From engine to tire, all parts mechanized
Are checked to high standards. Exclusive fees
For members only, often advertised
In posh neighbourhoods to use this garage
For expert and professional repair.
Line-ups are seldom with no over-charge
For waiting. Their attitude seems to care,
Which assures the owners of foreign cars.
Inside, there is a cafe that beats bars.

164. 'Today' Hooray!

Hooray for 'Today' paper, best layout
In the Far East, composed by nice, bright, young
Journalists, photographers, artists. Doubt
Not their intelligent minds, from far-flung
Schools and backgrounds. The hottest, latest news
Fresh of computers, cameras, and press.
From its '95 launching, staff enthuse
Its style and content, on par with the West.
All the older, established news compete
With its hip market. The most capable
Employees know it's the paper to beat!
Atmosphere is creative, sociable,
Informative. It's enjoyed by readers,
Who aspire to be the nation's leaders!

165. Chaps, Sirs

Large bookstores sprout in suburbs, character
Traps. Reading books is now hedonism
For people, owning a book a feather
In one's cap. No more the fatalism
Of torn or 'out' library books. Clientele
Browse books leisurely, quite nimble-minded
With contentment and coffee. Imbecile
Lookers watch people, often reminded
Watchers, readers differ in intellect.
Conversations once intelligible
Are now excerpts from books for the select
Who read. Clearly, these books are legible
In English. Each new book contains chapters
Which skimmed, can turn young chaps into wise sirs.

167. Blah Blah Black Sheep

Insomniacs can read or count sheep that bleat
Over an invisible fence. Breeding
Literate readers with books is a feat
Most book stores accomplish. Authors reading
Their latest works: novels, stories, poems
To journals are welcomed by listeners,
Who wander around searching as golems,
Starved clay figures, forming minds as readers.
Kitsilano's fashion flock walk West 4th
Shopping, browsing, strutting, meeting people.
From restaurants, clothes shops, they know the worth
Of goods. Commercial consciousness — staple
Trait of savvy, intellectual, hip sheep.
Books are absorbed even in their deep sleep...

168. Melancholic Alcoholic

Lost and dead loves deserve shrine memorials
Being companions in life's odyssey.
We pay respect attending funerals,
Wear black, mourn for years, in diplomacy.
Missing their loving camaraderie,
The atmosphere of mutual complaisance,
Our fond memories bring a reverie
Of good and bad times, even the nuisance.
To forget unsolved problems, inhuman
Treatment, we might empty the decanter
Of wine: from arguments with a woman,
Deaths, losses, loneliness, lack of banter,
Poverty – all these to melancholic
Madness, and with wine to alcoholic...

169. Victim Loser

Imee should have won the case. Empathy
For the accused defendant and envious
Legal workers who feared she'd win (pity
Was usually what they felt for previous
Victims) cause her to lose out of their spite.
Two other female employees had quit
The job because of the accused. The fight
Was lost from the start from his wealth. 'Defeat'
They thought,'A rich man? How dare they sue him
Having been poor and on welfare! Ingrates.'
A false witness friend covered up his whim
Of preying on young smart women on dates.
He offered five thousand to shut her din
But legal and co-workers saved his skin.

170. Flimsy Flim-Flam

The company recalls he could amble
Along to do his job. His black toupee
Was not an excuse for him to shamble
As a scalped Mohawk with an old teepee.
If the 3 Stooges on television
Didn't come on, he'd be a philanthropist
Volunteering helping on a mission.
But seeing bald men, a misanthropist
He became for his sanity. Moral:
"If you look like you saw a big monster,
You don't have to like people or floral
Things." He tried to keep his full time teamster
Job, but unhappy his toupee flim-flam
Made him quit relieved, since he was no sham.

171. Shanty Jaunt

A girl born on the poor side, jealousy
In her heart for the rich, also envy,
Living in a shanty, became hussy
Of the small town. Working without levy,
She saved up, ignoring the ridicule
And pity from Church. She compensated
Her depression with a daily capsule
Of 'speed' and for the money, she mated
With the wealthy wastrels. With her pander,
She held her head up above a hand-out.
On most week-days, the men would meander
To visit her in her hut. Each rich lout
Would pay his small fee, feeling quite jaunty,
Treating Cinderella in her shanty!

171. Shanty Jaunt

A girl born on the poor side, jealousy
In her heart for the rich, also envy,
Living in a shanty, became hussy
Of the small town. Working without levy,
She saved up, ignoring the ridicule
And pity from Church. She compensated
Her depression with a daily capsule
Of 'speed' and for the money, she mated
With the wealthy wastrels. With her pander,
She held her head up above a hand-out.
On most week-days, the men would meander
To visit her in her hut. Each rich lout
Would pay his small fee, feeling quite jaunty,
Treating Cinderella in her shanty!

172. Panel Discussion

The most intimate topics are discussed
For tv viewing audience. Privacy
Defeated by curiosity, disgust,
As the guests clamor for publicity.
Hostess presents the personal problems
Which trigger comments, advice from the crowd.
For society, family, these emblems
Represent disintegration aloud.
Perhaps, this may be a group therapy
For avid students of psychology?
Or could it be common philosophy
Known by experiences? Apology
To the discreet with secrets. These panels
Have no mercy in popular channels.

173. Knick Knacks

Apparently, the poetess had a knack
For nouns, verbs, beyond that of a peasant.
Fellow scribes were amazed enough to whack
Her head mentally, while seeming pleasant
To her face. She managed publication
From a home printer, with meritorious
Credits to her and partner. Elation
At their product made them feel victorious
Over enemies, critics. Amusement
At her muses, readers, analogy
Of a swan, she met with some bemusement,
Being humble. She thought,'Zymology
Can explain this success. Many knick-knacks
As yeast for grapes to wine, are bric-a-bracs.'

174. Blood and Love

Family and marriage are for faithful
Devotees, commonly called relatives
Who with love and kinship are dutiful,
Concerned with each other. Our daily lives
Run entwined, requiring tough stamina
To: accomplish tasks, plot successful schemes,
Weather storms (although our skins patina
May change), and realize our mutual dreams
Together. We are born with endurance
To last generations from forefather
To future children. Without forbearance,
We love conditionally each other.
As vital and strong as our own life blood
Our hearts, souls and minds strive for this great good!

175. Manager Mother

The first female a new infant has sight,
In the wonderful world of motherhood
Is her own. Delivery in limelight
At birth, with luck, skill, becomes livelihood.
When a woman's beauty depreciates
With time, her daughter's former dependence
On her as model does too. Appreciates
The daughter's beauty or independence
With her mother's close guiding excellence.
Ditto the girl's career if mother dotes
On her, supporting her every sentence
With maternal knowledge, wisdom and quotes.
She can rightly say with motherly pride
That, "Mothers daughters belong side by side."

176. Migrant Migraine

All nations have those who leave, emigrants
(Traitors) who escape future assassins,
Entering other lands as immigrants.
Adjusting to culture shock, aspirins
Are handy. Deluded, they're led astray
By brainwashing media of the country
Maybe half-truths lies which lured them away:
They may have better food in their pantry;
They might have just escaped strict martial law,
Or mean dictators diagnosing cancer;
Some left sunny climates for a snow thaw;
Some wed foreigners through a match-maker.
Differences may result in migraine
(From poison) or thinking matters mundane.

177. Diversity In University

Straight 'A's are signs of favouritism
Of students by teachers. Sorority
Practises a mild form of racism
Choosing members, as with fraternity.
Virgins may realize frigidity
In school though chivalry's historical.
Firm minds are developed. Rigidity
Is favoured, not unstable radical
Thought. Those few well schooled enter the Senate
Or Congress to be leaders tomorrow,
Promote liberty, unity, as fate
Decrees. Some fail exams, tests, with sorrow.
Some champion cultures and diversity.
Winners are made in university.

178. Gorgeous Poseur

The only reply was by happenstance
From someone as gorgeous. Infatuation
Is sneaky, it entraps one quite by chance.
Education is no cure. Graduation
Simply turns romance into cerebral
Attraction. It could be a delusion,
Wishing that from the star's centrifugal
Energy, arises an illusion
That I will be in touch with illustrious
Her. Perhaps, they're in some conspiracy
To bewitch me, alternating captious
Comments with remarks of accuracy?
In pursuing love, I must courageous
Be and prepare to be just as gorgeous.

179. Moslem Harem

In Islam, women can be concubines
Trained to serve willingly the infidels.
Women are guarded, within the confines
Protected by the cement citadels.
In the West, a grim gargoyle or griffin
Stands atop cathedrals. Polygamy
In the East is not even a bad sin.
To monogamous this is infamy.
Holy Wars in the past were fought to thwart
Such relationships. To teach vagabonds
Fidelity and love played a small part
In these Crusades. A holy person bonds
Longer, shines like a diamond diadem.
But infidelity runs each harem.

180. I.N.R.I.

'Infinitum Natum Rex Israel' --
Crucified, died, buried, risen as Christ,
Who healed the sick, fed the poor in travel.
His body, either stolen in a heist
Or appearing to Apostles, risen
From death. Attracting many followers
From all walks of life, He had twelve chosen
As His closest companions. Borrowers
Of His doctrine, they hope resurrection
Will usher in Heaven, a covenant
Of immortality. Revelation
Predicts cataclysms. Any remnant
Or survivor, as Genesis 12 tribes
Will live in New Jerusalem, notes scribes.

181. Popular Scholar

Books and notes accompany erudite
Students, who aspire to be sharp scholars,
A verbal discussion rather than fight
Preferable, not black/white but colours.
Life is lived by the devoted studious
In wisdom, intelligence, and virtue.
Real experience submerged for vicarious.
In truth, popularity should be due
To scholars, not only paper awards,
Trophies, but friends who with difficulty,
Know the value of playing with all cards.
Discerning members of the faculty
Agree smart students should be popular
And ignore the stupid who are polar.

182. Heckle and Hide

In some families, children are heckling
Siblings, playmates. In jest, they irritate
Those they love, wanting attention. Tickling
And teasing are not done with those they hate,
Although sadly, it can be a bother.
Perhaps, misunderstanding annoyance
Is the problem? Families can smother
Each other with affection, obeisance.
But ignoring someone is just as rude.
Sometimes it's a relief to disappear
From the tense scene, as a character booed
Off stage. Nervous tension is what we fear
Or a heart attack from constant, chronic
Irritation. Hiding may be tonic.

183. Mmm... Toes

He wanted hidden parts that were yummy,
Thinking,'Is it not more sinfully sweet
To eat delicacies for the tummy
That are as bound and covered as the feet?'
Girlfriends laughed at this wickedly kinky
Thought and punished him by wearing mens' shoes
Which hid them well. Like sucking a pinkie
Instead of the thumb, they kept hidden toes
From his eager eyes, but begged him to snack
On their fingers instead. He bought them rings
That fit their toes, bragging he had the knack
Of putting them on, taking off the things.
But though he badgered them for a nibble,
They denied him this pleasure by quibble.

184. Infinite Affinity

Destiny written in a cabala
Convinced the lovers that gnosticism
Was their path to salvation. Mandala
Circled their love and agnosticism
Was anathema to them. A requiem
Disturbed their ideas of corporeal.
Believing themselves immortal, mayhem
Was the only way an inimical
Act as death could part them. Although to pine
Away in such a resting position,
As corpses in cold hard coffins supine,
They thought that eternal invocation
Would be restful. Loving affinity
'Resting In Peace' into infinity...

185. Tabula Rasa

Infants are born in innocence. Erase
Past lives, as well parental influence
Till no memory leaves a mark nor trace
On the soul. A good or bad experience
Etches permanently spirits tablets,
Yet cross fingers, hope for a beginning.
Psychics can uncover all past snippets,
All deeds, words, thoughts, from blessing to sinning.
Some are trapped in dutiful cleanliness
Punished fro being ex-whores — a seance
Reveals. Some think it's next to godliness.
Others think surgeons are gods in science
And go under a murderous knife tool.
But our souls are never white as lamb's wool.

186. Lost Hearts

A symbol of love, a chain called anklet,
Traps willing prisoners in fine shackles.
More typical, round the wrist, a bracelet
With charms of love. Even thick-set ankles
Are worthy of these bonds without malice.
Two fall in love and some enter marriage,
Toasting their love with a drinking chalice.
A child is a bond, barring miscarriage.
Partners seek things for the intangible.
Sadly, things get lost, even precious gold
Though guarded, disappear as a bauble.
A treasured piece to exhibit love bold,
Brings pride of ownership. It's no gimmick
To display true love's gay trinkets, nor trick.

187. Juno's Joust

Marriage is worthy of Excalibur,
King Arthur's sword for defense. An attack
From enemies whatever caliber
Has to be defeated. A cul-de-sac
Situation with no way out alive
Could be avoided, just like any trap.
Goddess Juno could bless one if deprived
Of the bond. Lovers could probably wrap
Rings around fingers with divine blessings
From Hera. Protection with devotion
For mate and family is worth weddings
And ceremonies. Full of emotion,
One persists with each importunity,
Defending love requires integrity.

188. Your Hills And Valleys

Meandering round your esoteric
Lands, my will, resistance in erosion,
Excited by geography erotic!
Each step I take closer, a corrosion
From contact and sight of your luscious hills.
Discovering your secret lush valleys,
Lifts my searching soul with wondrous thrills!
Daily my eyes, mind or body dallies
Thirsting for your virginal quenching springs.
Fortune showers from your warm waterfalls,
As I stand below. Sun and moon shine brings
Light to curvy pathways. Your voice enthralls
My sad soul to sing that Heaven's rainbow
Leads me to walk true, wherever you go...

189. Secretive Secretary

Her boss needed a cool secretary,
Opinionated and informative
About the latest news. Mercenary
Business associates thought her secretive
Although gossip was her wide posterior
Large enough to be a motor rider
Made her stable, experienced, superior.
For these reasons, her lady boss chose her
As her personal aide. To embezzle
Companies she thought predestination
So she became intimate to sizzle
Her way to the top. A fibrillation
At her final scheme lost her, her big seat --
Of company secrets, she's indiscreet.

190. Inert Industry

At war's end, the army's small infantry
Were sent home having lost an inglorious
Battle. The wartime weapons industry
Which run the nation had no more precious
Metals, workers, to waste on this purpose.
Survivors who preferred peace, found solace
In the standstill. Female workers supposed
That this was God's wise decision and grace
And went back home to their kids, decrying
War and senseless murders, by the bad gun,
Which once put food on their tables. Crying
Ex-soldiers decided to have some fun
Instead and stayed home jobless and inert
Vowing to suntan, relax, not exert.

191. Salvaging Savage

Governments being hard, improvident
To poor citizens (considered lazy),
Beggars loiter urban streets, imprudent
Financially. Some are also crazy
Enough to look at the dumps, sort garbage:
Paper scraps, metals, glass, to recycle.
This occupation does not earn a wage.
It's as sinister as working in hell.
Ignorant poor people do the menial
Jobs, while educated find more secure
Labour. Statistics pretend denial
Of poverty, gloating when some endure
Tribulations, as those few who salvage
Human trash, wastes, as a modern savage.

192. Sweepstakes Journalism

The lottery office ran a charity
Clinic paid by the government sweepstakes.
A magazine covered winners, city
Dwellers who possibly were wealthy fakes
Interviewed in journalists articles.
Cover pages went to jackpot winners,
Who fortunate, gave in to some chuckles
From luck. Congratulatory dinners
Were served, as full colour cover photos
Were shot. The few monthly winning tickets
Published so readers would enter lottos.
There were suspicions officials pockets
Were illegally filled, but the journal
Ran days and this bad news was nocturnal.

193. Neighborhood Scars

As a girl, she entered neighborhood wars
Competing in childhood games and battle,
Which marked her tender skin with wounds and scars.
Noticing girls were docile as cattle,
She entered sports, until severe illness
Halted her short career with chicken pox.
There were not bullies nor bitches meanness
To fear, though she was cunning as a fox.
Young, she enjoyed playing various fun games,
Had few not-so-amusing accidents.
Boys and girls thought,'She's so friendly, she tames
All with her cute smiles. She seldom invents
Friends, tells lies, or gossips about the neighbors.
Her scars don't faze her and she seldom bores.'

194. Queen's B-Day

Each of the Queen's birthdays do celebrate
Her reign over the Queendom. Her birthday
On April 21st can liberate
Her Monarchists, as England on V-Day.
Winter's end ushers in the youthful Spring
Around this time. Refreshing rain showers
Water the earth's colourful blossoming
Forest, gardens, jungles, yards and flowers.
Her Royal magnitude inspires sonnets,
A tribute to Her charms. Of two hundred
Within, several are gems for coronets,
Decorations to ponder in the head.
Perhaps, a millennium poetry pageant
Will be held in her absence by regent?

195. Fantasies, Lies

With imagination, a pretty maid
Becomes beautiful. With mesmerism
She even becomes an ocean mermaid
With scales and fins. In anti-racism
Foreigners pretend to be more flippant
Than they are. In love, attractive moochers
Make holes in lovers pockets, though mordant
They might be. In fun, many lip smoochers
Steal moist kisses, without a forfeiture
Of their partners. In divorce, a forlorn
Mate may sue for alimony future.
Although she might be caught in-between torn
In half by unreal, foolish fantasies
Of better partners or living more lies.

196. Academy Awards

Annually golden statues called Oscars
Are handed out to the best new movies.
All the limos line up bringing the stars
To their destiny. Rivalry envies,
Seen in faces from losing the program,
With Oscars in hand as emcees announce
The winners. Is there possibly a scam
Involved when the wrong person wins? An ounce
Of doubt and suspicion with the onus
Of proof to the public. Actors chagrin
Defeated by judges votes. Sport bonus
To both losers an winners, who can grin
For media, promoting Academy
Honour through the grueling ceremony.

197. Caesar Salad

Famous men prefer a Caesar salad
With their meals. Though Rome burned, fiddled Nero
To the mad public an insane ballad.
All can vote in democracy – hero
Or no hero. Justice, rights, rules and laws
Guide power, hierarchies and politics.
Candidates must have qualities and jaws
To compete. Some do enjoy theatrics,
Performing live, on video, cinema,
Using media to reach educated
Voters. Gladiators fight in arena,
Hoping to win over rivals. Hated
Men lose the battles, bowing to Caesar
Who watches men from above and afar...

198. isarte

Creative females want to be artists
To express emotions and ideas.
Some struggling with technique, being realists
Attend courses, workshops with videos
In various media, such as internet
Are viewable to the public, who surf
Network waves. One such user 'isarte' met
Many strangers. Some had websites or turf.
This artist is mistress of conception
Exhibiting drawings in coffee shops,
Churches, centers. Welcoming reception
Of fame, fortune, she constantly name drops
Other artists, celebrities. Her art
May be unknown but she has soul and heart.

199. Cat And Alcoholic

Sorrows befell her sad life, the prefect
Of a Christian girls school. Her pet cat's purr
Following her daily rounds made perfect
Music to her ears. 'My prize feline cur
Pleases with its fine high tones. Our soft couch
Invites us nightly to rest, with aged wine,
A warm shower, a snack... a supine slouch
And soon bliss and rest. My cat's meow and whine
Stir my soul. Vibrating ease and comfort
Reverberates through its chest, as we lie
Close – two lonely souls, my faithful consort
And I. Peaceful harmony with each sigh
As we caress hand and paw.' Catholic
Heaven at home, cat and alcoholic...

200. Return Of Jodi

In outer space, where humanity's doom
Is foretold in movies science fiction,
Lives a heroine who conquers this gloom
With her education and clear diction.
She flies around in a high-tech stagecraft
With her knowledge. The evil Dark Ages
Of cinema, once the field of each daft
Dolt, violent criminal who enrages
Watchers, now falls under the spell of 'Nell' --
A victim who triumphs within reason.
The 'Accused' and 'Silence' sound the death knell
Of evil, ending criminals treason
Against law and order. So , may the Force
Be with her and may she avoid the worst.

1. Coronets & Bonnets
2. Bastard Bowdlerism
3. Willing Wittols
4. Visiting The Queen
5. American Lioness
6. Honey Bear
7. Maestro's Muses
8. Royal Sun
9. Marrying In Faith
10. Romantic Dilettante
11. Fluttery-by Valentine
12. Fine Dahlia
13. Eulogy For A Eunuch
14. Sisterhood Brotherhood Collusion
15. Queen's Deponent
16. Domesticated Meek
17. Gangster Moll
18. Victim's Complaint
19. Humiliation Humbles
20. Love's Dialectic
21. Queen Of Hoi Polloi
22. Holy Yokel
23. Gossiping Women
24. Friend Enemy
25. Choices Of Temptations
26. Domestics Muse
27. Family Birthright
28. Written Laundry
29. Wet Dream
30. Island Hospitality*
31. Border Crossings
32. Shattered North
33. Impatient Waiting
34. Jealousy's Gargoyle
35. Loneliness Of Lovelessness
36. Housekeeping Husband
37. Royal Tea
38. Modern Aunt
39. alt.showbiz.gossip
40. Eczema Of Love
41. Love's Diamond
42. IT Girls
43. Christian Empress
44. Hope From The Pope
45. One-Legged Nun
46. Group Date
47. Artists Loft
48. Creative Luck
49. Beauty's Fool
50. Poncho Honcho

Editor's Choice Award May 2001, International Library of Poetry

51. Eccentric Priest
52. Humble Will
53. Almighty Parents
54. Pygmy Philosophy
55. History's Paradox
56. Moths To Flames
57. Domestic Enterprise
58. Victory To Victims
59. Family Prayers
60. Chicken Gibbet
61. Lewd Prude
62. Braille Braggadocio
63. Meteoric Nights
64. Yogi Bearah
65. Victims Vindication
66. Tit For Tat
67. Breathing Same Air
68. Family Lunacy
69. Echo Recollection
70. Sideburns In Suburbia
71. Funny Foster Home
72. Burger Buns
73. Desert Gambling
74. Gore Vs. Bush
75. Nell In A Shell
76. Spic 'N Span
77. Lady Banshee
78. Lovers Limericks
79. Bimbo Cat
80. Telepathetic
81. Puppet Parody
82. Shy Pyromaniac
83. Wicked Wicca
84. Cruel Crusades
85. Anna And Red King
86. Windows & Gates
87. Peaches & Cream
88. E-Romance
89. Foreign Zealot
90. Expo '86
91. European Journey
92. Heathen In Eden
93. Vegetarian Egalitarian
94. Gas Man
95. Muscle Women
96. Fanatic Crowd
97. Fave Things
98. Art & Community
99. Copy Cat
100. Minorities Dilemma

101. Good-bye Muses
102. Vegetarian Science
103. Ugly Photos
104. Cocaine Insanity
105. Bawdy Lair
106. Bacon & Ham
107. Spanish Stumble
108. Venus Flytrap
109. Suburban Doldrums
110. Neuphoria Club
111. Bally-hoo
112. Hollywood Establishment
113. Feminism Herstory
114. Haunting House
115. Hyperbolic Lecturer
116. Grunge Gal Pals
117. Crumpled Paper
118. Coffee Morning
119. Badminton Baguio
120. Tempestuous Temp
121. Holy Rood
122. Seconds In Love & Out
123. Ewe
124. Court Her
125. Titanic Heroin
126. Hungry Bear
127. Bitches On Beaches
128. Ethnic City
129. Grumbleweeds
130. Clay Feet On Pedestal
131. Crows In Council
132. Healthy Canajuns
133. Star's Idiosyncrasy
134. Joe Jacamar
135. Matron Patron
136. Nasty Nickelodeon
137. No Smoking
138. Princess Margarine
139. Mother Bee
140. Rumour Humor
141. The 7 Suzaras
142. Farewell Welfare
143. Maid & Her Queen
144. Dr. Cosmetic
145. Scary Scars
146. Silent Lambastes
147. Marcos Martial Law
148. DWA
149. Social Medical Housework
150. Actress & Queen

151. Prayer For Pregnancy
152. Hoity Toity
153. Tarot Truths
154. Cowabunga
155. Coo-coo Bird
156. Salome Saigon
157. Squeaky Bed
158. MacDonna
159. Sir Womanizer
160. Fil-Veterans
161. Grudge Of A Drudge
162. Dull House
163. Gee Cats
164. Today Hooray!
165. Chaps, Sirs
166. Noble Barn
167. Blah Blah Black Sheep
168. Melancholic Alcoholic
169. Victim Loser
170. Flimsy Flim-flam
171. Shanty Jaunt
172. Panel Discussion
173. Knick-Knacks
174. Blood & Love
175. Manager Mother
176. Migrant Migraine
177. Diversity University
178. Gorgeous Poseur
179. Moslem Harem
180. I.N.R.I.
181. Popular Scholar
182. Heckle & Hyde
183. Mmm... Toes
184. Infinite Affinity
185. Tabula Rasa
186. Lost Hearts
187. Juno Joust
188. Hills and Valleys
189. Secretive Secretary
190. Inert Industry
191. Salvaging Savage
192. Sweepstakes Journalism
193. Neighbourhood Scars
194. Queen's B-Day
195. Fantasies, Lies
196. Academy Awards
197. Caesar Salad
198. isARTe
199. Cat And Alcoholic
200. Return Of Jodi